# EVERY TEACHER'S GUIDE TO
# CLASSROOM MANAGEMENT

Written by Alice Ter

D0624705

Editor: Karen P. Hall

Illustrator: Darcy Tom

Project Director: Carolea Williams

CTP © 1997 Creative Teaching Press, Inc., Cypress, CA 90630

# TABLE OF CONTENTS

# INTRODUCTION

*Every Teacher's Guide to Classroom Management* offers a wide assortment of practical, easy-to-implement classroom management techniques for both new and experienced teachers. Whether you're looking for time-saving tips, suggestions for setting up your classroom, ways to organize and store supplies, or successful communication strategies, this comprehensive guide will help you reach all your professional goals.

This guide is divided into five sections—*Time, People, Space, Materials,* and *Paperwork*—each beginning with a general overview and ending with a quick-check review. Also included is a handy resource section to help you implement classroom management procedures simply and easily.

*Time Management* helps maximize productivity while planning and teaching lessons. This section includes:

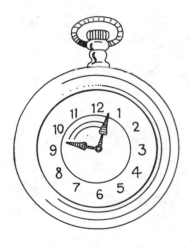

- guidelines for setting and achieving goals.
- personal planning-time pointers.
- ways to use "wait time."
- quick and creative classroom routines.
- ways to simplify time-consuming tasks.

*People Management* offers communication strategies for creating a productive and supportive classroom community. This section includes:

- beginning-of-the-year activities.
- ways to accomodate different learning modalities.
- methods for assigning and monitoring student jobs.
- ways to establish positive communication with students.
- techniques for monitoring student progress.
- ways to help students establish good study habits.
- games and activities that teach students responsibility.
- methods for dealing with inappropriate behavior.
- ways to communicate student progress to parents.
- tips for working with assistants and volunteers.

*Space Management* discusses various ways to set up and use classroom space effectively. This section includes:

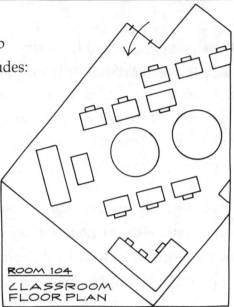

ROOM 104
CLASSROOM
FLOOR PLAN

- classroom floor plans.
- suggested seating arrangements.
- flexible furniture ideas.
- furniture arrangements to accommodate different learning modalities.
- how to set up your personal work space.
- unique ways to use "hidden" classroom space.
- ideas for practical bulletin-board displays.

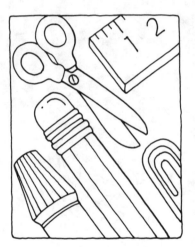

*Materials Management* provides a large variety of storage and distribution strategies to create an organized learning environment. This section includes:

- suggested supplies to store in the classroom.
- ways to collect free or inexpensive classroom materials.
- simple methods to organize classroom materials.
- easy and inexpensive storage systems.
- ways to manage use of materials in the classroom.

*Paperwork Management* discusses "practice without paper" teaching techniques and efficient filing systems to reduce paperwork hassles. This section includes:

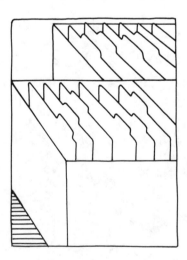

- teaching techniques that reduce paperwork.
- self-correcting and partner-checking techniques for students.
- efficient record-keeping systems.
- how to label and organize files for easy retrieval.
- important files to keep in the classroom.
- ways to organize and manage teacher mail.

# TIME MANAGEMENT

Time is a unique and important resource. We cannot increase the time we have, nor can we shorten it. It is up to you how to use and prioritize time each day.

As a teacher, it is important to be an effective time manager, allocating time to plan and teach lessons, perform extracurricular activities, and accomplish personal goals. Through the use of simple time-management techniques, you can successfully accomplish both your professional and personal goals more efficiently. By planning carefully, examining your objectives, and prioritizing tasks, you will discover a unique principle—you can work smarter, not harder, and discover hours in the day you never knew you had.

## In this chapter, you will

- assess your time-management practices.

- gain practical time-management tips.

- discover how to set and achieve goals.

- discover how to streamline classroom routines.

- increase the effectiveness of your time-management practices.

*" How pleasant it is, at the end of the day,*
*No follies to have to repent;*
*But reflect on the past, and be able to say,*
*That my time has been properly spent. "*
*—Jane Taylor*

# Setting and Achieving Goals

**Writing daily goals helps us organize and use time more efficiently.** When goals are not written down, they often dissolve into a wish list which is soon shed like an old skin. The pressures of the day justify the lack of accomplishment and we simply forget to complete various tasks.

Use the Daily Planner (reproducible, page 111) to write your daily "to-do" lists, and include the steps needed to reach your goals—they are your course of action each day. Using "to-do" lists to organize and compartmentalize your daily tasks helps you lower stress, reduce the amount of work you take home, and work more efficiently toward your goals. Consider the following steps when preparing and completing "to-do" lists.

- Brainstorm both short- and long-term goals.

- Break down long-term goals into small, manageable steps.

- Save the most difficult tasks for your peak productivity time—those hours in which you do your best critical thinking and problem solving. You can double your productivity and save time by accommodating your natural body clock.

- Organize and group your objectives into categories such as *Paperwork, Office Errands,* and *People Contacts.*

- Assign time blocks for completing each group of tasks, then work on one goal at a time. Research shows that for most jobs, we function more efficiently by completing one task before moving on to the next.

- Write tasks on stick-on notes and attach them to your lesson-plan book to monitor your progress throughout the day.

*Paperwork*
MORNING
1. Fill out health-insurance questionnaire.
2. Grade science papers.
3. Review state reports.

*Office Errands*
BREAK
1. Gather supplies for science project.
2. Pick up first-aid supplies.

*Social Tasks*
AFTER SCHOOL
1. Talk to Angela about olympic program.
2. Talk to Crescent about math groups.
3. Call parent volunteers.

Daily Planner
Oct. 7
✓ = um.    • = mmm
Things to do before school:
☐ Fill out health insurance questionnaire.
☐ Grade science papers.
→ = mmm
Things to do at school in the morning:
☐ Gather supplies for science project.
☐ Pick up first-aid supplies.
Things to do at school in the afternoon:
☐ Talk to Angela about Olympic program.
☐ Talk to Crescent about math groups.
Things to do after school:
☐ Call parent volunteers.
☐

# Personal Planning Time

**Set aside time each day for quiet, uninterrupted work periods.** Protecting your planning time is important—when interrupted, you lose that time as well as time needed to regain your focus.

It is imperative that you set boundaries for effective time management. Be polite and tactful to others, but draw the line. Learn to differentiate urgent requests from those that can be addressed another time. Although it is admirable to help students, parents, and colleagues, limits are needed—the stress and frustration of not having time to complete your own goals will, in the long run, affect both your work performance and your ability to support others.

Post a schedule listing times you're available. Hang a sign on your closed classroom door when you need quiet, undisturbed work time. Notify others that you are unavailable and offer alternative times to meet. Discuss with students when it is appropriate and inappropriate to interrupt your work period. Ask office personnel to take phone messages during planning and preparation periods, and return phone calls when your work is complete.

**Weekly Schedule**

| | MONDAY | TUESDAY | WEDNESDAY | THURSDAY | FRIDAY |
|---|---|---|---|---|---|
| 8:30-9:30 | READING | | | | → |
| 9:30-10:15 | LANGUAGE ARTS | | | | → |
| 10:15-10:30 | RECESS | (Teacher | Available) | | → |
| 10:30-11:00 | LIBRARY | COMPUTERS | MUSIC | COMPUTERS | MUSIC |
| 11:00-12:00 | MATH | | | | → |
| 12:00-12:30 | LUNCH | Personal | Planning | Time | → |
| 12:30-1:30 | SCIENCE | SOCIAL STUDIES | SCIENCE | SOCIAL STUDIES | SCIENCE |
| 1:30-2:45 | ART | PE | ART | PE | WEEKLY REVIEW |
| 2:45-3:30 | TEACHER AVAILABLE | | TEACHER AVAILABLE | | |

# Time-Saving Techniques

One of the keys to effective time management is eliminating time wasters—tasks that consume your time with little or no return value. To use your time more efficiently, share and exchange responsibilities with your colleagues. Delegate tasks to students, paraprofessionals, or volunteers. Divide complex projects into manageable pieces, and set time limits. Establish a consistent routine—systematic planning and positive action will help you organize your day and reclaim lost minutes and hours.

## What to Do While You Wait

- You arrive at a meeting early—Bring a stack of papers to grade, envelopes to address, and papers to file.

- You're waiting for parents to arrive for conferences—Perform tasks that are easily adjustable to interruptions, such as changing a bulletin board, organizing a drawer, filing papers, or writing a quick note.

- The assembly does not start on time—Review with students your last lesson or homework for that night, or play word- and number-guessing games.

- Students are waiting in line—Use extra minutes for instruction such as reviewing times tables or spelling words, asking riddles about current subject matter, teaching sign language, and so on.

# Timely Teaching Tips

- Invite students to create and put up bulletin boards rather than spending extensive time creating teacher-made materials. A few letters may be crooked, but it will save you hours, and your students will enjoy and learn from the experience.

- Don't laminate everything. It may be easier and less time-consuming to have students help make new materials.

- Instead of shopping for and wrapping individual gifts, let students choose from a basket of inexpensive paperback books for birthdays or special occasions.

- Select only some student work to grade. It is not necessary to collect and grade all practice papers. Invite students to self-check and grade their own work using an answer key. Even if a few mistakes are made, it will save you time and be a great learning experience for your students.

- Set up a grading table and enlist the help of paraprofessionals (paid assistants) and parent volunteers.

- Recruit parent volunteers to help with "out-of-the-classroom" tasks such as photo-copying notices, writing directions for classroom games and activities, and cleaning art smocks.

- Recruit a qualified individual, not connected with the school, to proofread all parent communications.

- Use "practice-without-paper" techniques such as student chalkboards, hand signals, computers, calculators, and games.

## Creative Classroom Routines that Save Time

- Use a clothesline to take attendance. Label clothespins with students' personal numbers (see *Personal Numbering System*, page 91), then attach them to a clothesline in numerical order. When students arrive in the morning, have them remove their clothespins and place them in a box. Ask a student monitor to list absentees on a yellow stick-on note (record clothespins still attached) and leave the note on your desk.

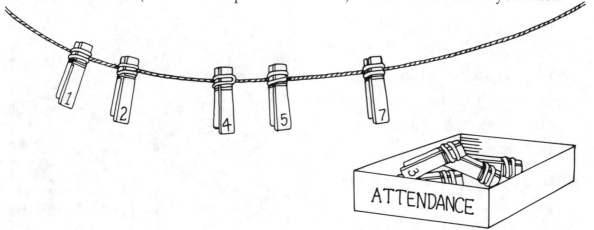

- Collect completed class work by asking students to place their papers in holding trays, file folders, or work slots/cubbies, then check off their personal numbers from a laminated class list posted nearby. Use the list to dismiss students for recess, calling out the personal numbers of those who have completed their work.

- Have student helpers or parent volunteers use labeled work slots/cubbies to distribute corrected papers without disturbing the class.

- Use cardboard desktop clocks to remind students of important appointments such as when to leave the room for special classes or early dismissal for a doctor's visit. Write the departure times on the clocks, and attach them to individual student's desks. Encourage students to remind each other when it's time for their appointments.

- Assign "study buddies" to compile work packets for absent partners. Store several construction-paper folders and cover sheets (see Welcome Back! reproducible, page 112) in holding trays. Ask buddies to collect assignments, place them inside the folders, and list makeup assignments on cover sheets.

- Use a stopwatch and a "puppet helper" to play Beat the Clock during transitions from one lesson to the next. Make your expectations explicit (e.g., no movement unless it is part of the transition; no one can ask for help during this time). Use the puppet to clarify directions, give the signal to start timing, and cheer students' progress.

- Have students place completed homework folders in the appropriate holding tray upon entering the room each morning and check off their personal number from a check-off list posted nearby. Ask homework monitors to arrange completed homework chronologically using personal numbers, check work for completion, place the check-off sheet on top, and set the stack in a central holding tray. Have the monitors list on the chalkboard the personal numbers of students missing homework.

## Time-Consuming Tasks Made Simple

- Store art materials on a rolling cart, and assign student helpers to distribute needed materials before the lesson while the class is involved in other activities or at recess.

- Once a week, have helpers distribute corrected work while classmates clean out their desks. Or, designate bins for students to pick up corrected work as they leave at the end of the day.

- Have students help complete tasks as they talk to you during recess—organize the paper drawer, distribute supplies for the next lesson, feed classroom pets, and so on.

- Write sentences for oral-language practice on overhead transparencies or sentence strips, and file for future use.

- Keep a supply list taped to your file cabinet. Any time you think of a needed supply, jot it down. Then, at the beginning or end of each school day, make one trip to the supply closet to collect needed materials.

# Time Management Review

## Did you:

 write daily "to-do" lists, scheduling more challenging tasks during your peak productivity times?

 minimize interruptions during prep time by notifying others of your schedule and clearly defining your boundaries?

 eliminate time wasters by delegating responsibilities, collaborating with colleagues, and taking advantage of "wait time"?

☑ streamline your efforts by following established classroom routines and simplifying general tasks?

*" He who every morning plans the transactions for the day and follows out that plan, carries a thread that will guide him through the labyrinth of the most busy life. "*

*—Victor Hugo*

# PEOPLE MANAGEMENT

Teachers are people managers. They teach students from diverse backgrounds a common core of knowledge, and prepare them to face life's challenges. As professional communicators, teachers network and interact with parents, classroom volunteers, colleagues, support personnel, supervisors, paraprofessionals, and members of the community. Motivating others to do their personal best is the quintessential task. Communication is the key. Caring is the connection.

Through the use of simple people-management skills, you can create a caring, productive classroom environment. By building trust, setting clear guidelines, and providing positive reinforcement, your students will be confident, task-oriented people who are motivated and excited about learning.

## In this chapter, you will

- discover ways to create a supportive and inclusive classroom community.

- learn to establish trust with students.

- investigate important motivational strategies.

- discover how to encourage responsible behavior.

- determine effective interventions when students misbehave.

- gain techniques for communicating and collaborating with parents, colleagues, and paraprofessionals.

*" Personal relationships are the fertile soil from which all advancement, all success, all achievement in real life grows. "*
—*Ben Stein*

# Building a Classroom Community

**The need to belong is felt by all people, including students from diverse backgrounds.** Students who feel accepted and valued by both the teacher and their peers are more likely to perform well in school. As you establish a caring classroom community, consider how you verbally and nonverbally communicate with students—what you say, how you express your thoughts, your body language, and the consistency of your actions. By displaying genuine feelings of interest and concern, you will motivate students to do their very best.

## Getting to Know Families

Initiate contact with students' families within the first week of school, preferably the first day. Parents will appreciate your interest in their child, and students will feel more welcome knowing you care about their lives. The information you obtain from this initial contact (and those that follow) helps clarify the concerns and needs of your students.

Send home the Let's Get Acquainted! form (reproducible, page 113) to learn more about your students and their families. Relieve first-week jitters by inviting students to share information about their families. Save "get acquainted" forms and use them for conversation starters during initial phone calls to parents or on Back-to-School Night. File forms in individual student folders for future reference.

## Getting to Know Students

During the first week of school, play a variety of games that help students get acquainted and feel part of a supportive team.

**What's in a Name?**  Investigate and discuss name origins. Compare how letter sounds differ in certain languages (e.g., the Spanish letter *J* as in Juan sounds like the letter *H*). Invite students to make an ABC book of classmates' names and what they mean in different languages. For example, *Alice* becomes *Alicia* in Spanish, which means "truth."

**People Search.**  Write and photocopy statements pertaining to students' hobbies, interests, and physical descriptions. Invite students to locate classmates who match their descriptions, writing names alongside each statement.

**Name Search.** Make word-search puzzles containing students' names (see Name Search reproducible, page 114). Have students write names vertically, horizontally, or diagonally, one letter per box, filling empty squares with random letters. Invite students to trade papers and search for each name.

**Portrait Puzzles.** Invite students to draw self-portraits on construction paper, and write several facts about themselves on the back. Have them cut portraits into puzzle pieces and place them in resealable plastic bags. Collect and randomly redistribute puzzles. Have students put puzzles together to identify classmates, then turn puzzle pieces over and reassemble to reveal written facts.

**Name Graph.** In advance, make a bar graph on butcher paper. Place letters of the alphabet on the horizontal axis and numbers on the vertical axis. Begin by asking if there is anyone in the class whose first name begins with *A*. Have those students stand up and introduce themselves, taking turns saying their names as the rest of the class echoes a greeting. After each introduction, have the student write his or her name in the appropriate box on the graph. After all *A* names are written, invite those students to stand up together while classmates try to recall and recite names from memory. (The graph can be used for help as needed.) Continue with other letters of the alphabet until all students have introduced themselves.

Extensions:

- Have students write their names on stick-on notes and attach them to the class graph when corresponding letters are called.

- Graph students' names according to the number of letters in their names.

- Prepare individual graphs for students to fill out while you complete the enlarged version.

| | A | B | C | D | E |
|---|---|---|---|---|---|
| **6** | | | | | |
| **5** | | | | | |
| **4** | | | Cher | | |
| **3** | | | Carmelita | Doris | |
| **2** | Amy | Bart | Connie | Dan | Elliott |
| **1** | Andy | Bobbie | Cassie | Dawn | Ellen |

## Supporting Different Learning Modalities

Vary instructional strategies so activities validate different learning modalities (audio, visual, tactile, kinesthetic), and encourage positive peer interaction. Recognize each individual learner and support his or her own unique style of receiving and expressing information. Promote acceptance and inclusion in your classroom by using "promising practices"—procedures and techniques focusing on *how* students learn as opposed to *what* they learn.

- Follow verbal instructions with visual cues and hands-on applications. Work with manipulatives to clarify and validate learning. Many students need to "see" and "do" before comprehending new concepts.

- When teaching a lesson, have students reread concepts being taught using modified or revised text. For example, enlarge or rewrite text to simplify important concepts or add more challenging vocabulary.

- Provide learning centers with multi-leveled activities addressing various learning styles. Permit students to move through centers at their own pace. Provide materials such as tape recorders and manipulatives to encourage audio and tactile learners.

- Let students choose how to apply what they learn by encouraging verbal communication and hands-on projects in addition to paperwork. Students feel comforted knowing there is more than one way to succeed. For example, let a student tape-record a story or report rather than write it.

- Collaborate with teachers who accompany special-needs students. Permit students who cannot write to dictate to a collaborating teacher or assistant, or record their answers on audiotape.

- Assign "study buddies" to encourage cooperation and provide assistance to students needing help. With parent permission, invite buddies to exchange phone numbers.

## Assigning Classroom Responsibilities

A simple and effective way to build a supportive, inclusive classroom community is to have students assist with the daily operations of your classroom. Students will feel a sense of purpose and pride by performing classroom duties. Refer to Appendix A (pages 126–127) for a list of classroom leadership jobs to incorporate into your classroom.

Be sure to reward students for jobs well done through personalized thank-you notes, homework passes, computer time, and so on. Assign job "favorites" to students displaying exceptional effort, or invite top performers to select their own jobs. Motivate students to perform classroom duties by sharing success stories of influential leaders, emphasizing how these individuals served and assisted others. For added fun, invite older students to apply for specific jobs by filling out application forms and interviewing for positions.

## Ways to Assign and Manage Student Jobs

**Job Pockets.** Write titles or draw pictures of classroom jobs on library-book pockets. Place student name cards inside each pocket to assign responsibilities. Rotate name cards to assign new jobs. Have students write job titles on the back of each card to monitor tasks performed throughout the year. Change popular, easily-trainable job assignments daily or weekly. All other jobs may be assigned by the month or quarter.

**Job Wheel.** Connect two tagboard circles, one four inches (10 cm) smaller than the other, with a large brad. Use a permanent marker to divide the smaller circle into pie-shaped wedges, then write student names in each one. Write job titles on outer-circle sections and align with student names. Assign new jobs by rotating the inner circle.

**Helping Hands.** Use the Helping Hands reproducibles (pages 115–116) to create an adorable student job board. Write job titles on separate construction-paper circles. Photocopy, cut out, color, and attach centipede parts to create a bulletin-board display. Write student names on centipede hands and pin them to the body to assign jobs. (You may choose to use more than one "arm" per circle for partner jobs.) Change jobs by moving centipede hands.

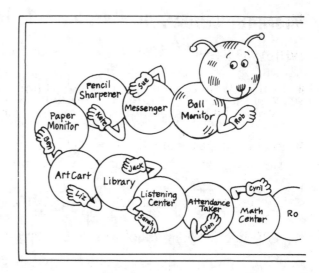

## Getting Feedback from Students and Colleagues

Most teachers realize the importance of positive feedback, yet do not always consistently practice it in the classroom. To determine how much positive feedback you give, invite peers and/or students to assess and evaluate your performance. Have a colleague take notes or videotape you while you teach. Ask him or her to provide feedback on your interactions with students, including suggestions for improvement. Invite students to fill out a teacher report card, evaluating your performance in different areas. (You may choose to make a questionnaire for students to complete.) Having students submit evaluations anonymously encourages honest feedback, and you will empower them by acting on their suggestions.

# Show You Care . . .

## With Words:

- Be friendly and patient. Give yourself time out when angry or upset. Students react more to the tones of your voice than the words being spoken.

- Avoid using sarcasm. Students may misinterpret it as criticism or jokes at their expense.

- Give encouraging feedback. Emphasize the positive, and always acknowledge effort.

- Express confidence in student capabilities. Success is related more to "I can" than IQ.

- Be honest—students appreciate direct yet gentle feedback.

- Regularly praise student performance, both publicly and privately. Remember, good behavior that is ignored tends to disappear.

## With Actions:

- Remember to smile. Show students you genuinely enjoy their presence.

- Give students your undivided attention. Avoid doing other work (sorting papers, communicating with colleagues) while students are speaking.

- Always make eye contact when speaking to students—four to six seconds per glance (about the time it takes to click a camera). Eye contact shows you are focused and interested in what's being said.

- Watch your body language. Keep arms to your sides rather than crossed in front of you. Crossing your arms as you speak or listen may be misconstrued as anger or impatience.

- Follow through with promises. Students learn to trust your words when actions follow.

- Be consistent in your behavior. Students feel more secure and safe when expectations and boundaries are clearly established.

# MBWA: Management by Walking Around

**Circulating around the classroom and monitoring progress is the key to keeping students focused on learning.** Use the following guidelines as you interact with students during initial instruction, distributed practice sessions, and cooperative or learning-center activities.

- Interact with students on a one-to-one basis.

- Offer immediate, positive feedback.

- Assist students in a timely manner.

- Discourage off-task behavior by standing close to the disruptive student.

- Reinforce understanding by providing private, personal assistance.

## Steps to Monitoring Seatwork

### Step 1—Once Through Quickly

After giving assignments to students, immediately begin to circulate and monitor progress. Make an initial "sweep" of the classroom as students begin their work. Check if every student or group has the necessary materials to complete the assignment. Specifically state what you will be looking for as you circulate. For example, *I'll be moving around quickly this morning to check that you are all on page 32, have two sharpened pencils, and a calculator.* This initial step is essential no matter what teaching strategy you use. Once students focus on learning, you are ready to proceed to the next step.

### Step 2—Praise, Prompt, and Move On

After you complete a quick sweep, tell students two specific accomplishments you will be looking for as you circulate the room a second time. For example, *I will be looking to see if your name and personal number are on your paper, and I will be looking at the first few answers to see if you are able to distinguish between obtuse and acute angles.* As you monitor progress, offer specific praise for accuracy. Keep comments quick and concise; guide students to success rather than solving the problems for them. Listen to your intuition— you will know when one student can solve a problem independently and when another will need more support. Prompt students needing help, then proceed on to other students, making a mental note to return to those who experienced difficulty. Watch the clock—you may tend to stay too long with a particular student which can create dependency. Remember to assist and praise all students, including those who listen to and understand concepts the first time.

### Step 3—The Three-Stop Check

Continue to monitor and assist students throughout independent practice. Be on the lookout for general confusion or misunderstanding. If you find yourself stopping three times in just one section of the classroom to help students with the same problem, take a quick survey to determine how many others are having difficulty. If only a few students raise their hands, form a small group with these individuals and reteach the concept again. If many students are experiencing the same confusion, reteach some or all of the lesson to the entire class, using different examples and checking for understanding.

### Step 4—Record Progress

Record mastery of skills as you monitor progress at the end of the work period. Using graph paper, list students' names on the vertical axis and skills along the horizontal axis. Mark +, −, or ? to indicate whether a student understands, partially understands, or does not understand a concept. As soon as possible, set aside time to reteach concepts to individuals or small groups.

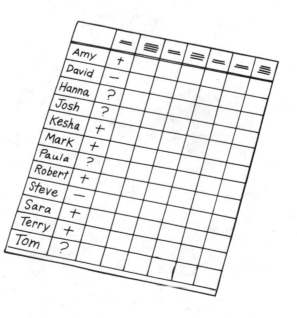

## Nonverbal Monitoring Techniques

Monitoring becomes more efficient through skilled, nonverbal communication. Eye contact, degrees of proximity, and unpredictable movement can enable you to keep all students on task as you offer one-to-one assistance to those needing it most. Consider some of the following techniques to monitor work progress in your classroom.

**Scan the Room Continually.**  Scan the classroom with your eyes and ears. Use eye contact to acknowledge effort and achievement. Always be aware of what is happening in the classroom, and deal quickly with any signs of misbehavior. Effective managers can work in one classroom area and oversee another with just a look or signal.

**Get Closer to Off-Task Students.**  The closer you are to students, the more appropriate their behavior will be. If a student is acting out during guided or independent practice, stop directly in front of the student, look into his or her eyes, and quietly wait for him or her to correct the behavior. If you are teaching and a student is misbehaving, simply move closer to that student without stopping the lesson. Your presence alone or a gentle touch on the shoulder will encourage him or her back on task.

**Use Unpredictable Movement.**  Vary where you stand and observe student performance from different parts of the classroom. When giving instruction, move periodically so students originally in the back of the classroom or off to the sides are in direct line of vision. Students get on-task more quickly knowing that the rotation pattern is random.

**Use the Flag System.**  Teach your students to use a "flag" signal when they need assistance. Make flags using laminated tagboard and brads, and tape them to student desks. When students need help, have them raise flags instead of their hands—this allows them to continue their work rather than frantically waving to get your attention. If you are already assisting a student, ask those waiting for help to complete other problems, rethink the one causing difficulty, or read until you are available.

# Developing Good Study Habits

**Students are more likely to take responsibility for their learning when encouraged to set personal goals and pace their own work.** To help students reach their goals and establish good study habits, clearly communicate your expectations from day one. Communicate explicitly what each activity, procedure, or skill should look like when complete. Have students use self-evaluation forms (reproducibles, pages 117–124) to self-monitor progress. Set up personalized conferences to give positive feedback, assess understanding of concepts, and encourage progress. Guide students to choose goals that are realistic, measurable, and have a target date. Finally, model responsibility to students by following through with promises, completing your "homework" on time, and acknowledging mistakes and errors.

## Helping Students Set Goals

- Have students estimate and compare time needed to complete various tasks. Use the Estimating Accomplishments reproducible (page 117) to help students estimate and compare time needed to complete whole-group and independent activities such as sustained silent reading, solving math problems, or cleaning up art supplies. Invite students to share their results and brainstorm ways to improve their time. Give them the opportunity to repeat the tasks within a few weeks to see if they can improve.

- Invite students to keep Personal Learning Logs (reproducible, page 118). Have them write each goal with expected completion dates. Ask students to monitor and record progress, brainstorming ways to improve their performance and reach their goals. Have students record daily work goals on the Daily Work Goals sheet (reproducible, page 119), or write goals on stick-on notes and attach them to desktops as visual reminders.

- Have students maintain Choosing Time Journals (reproducible, page 120), recording self-selected activities. Encourage students to share their experiences, comparing short-term gratification (playing a computer game) to long-term satisfaction (working to finish a book report early).

Choosing Time Journal

Name Sara Smith
Date 1/20

My choice is
Computer math game

I choose this because

## Achieving Goals through "Backward Planning"

Responsibility is an abstract concept to students, particularly when it involves long-term projects. Backward planning is a concrete time-management procedure that involves setting a final due date for a particular task, dividing the task into smaller parts, and determining separate due dates for each part. The process actually involves counting backward to assign due dates for each part of the task. The goal is to complete a long-term assignment in an organized and timely fashion. Use the following steps to help you teach backward planning to your students.

1. **Give every student a packet of calendar months needed for planning, and have them star the final due date with a red marker.** Have students fill out Backward Planning forms (reproducible, page 121) to make calendar pages for one trimester. Ask the class to decide on a due date for an assignment (e.g., a book report) and star the date on their calendars. Be certain the due date does not fall on a student-free day or holiday, and that students allow you enough time to correct and record grades before report cards are due.

| | | | DECEMBER | | | |
|---|---|---|---|---|---|---|
| SUNDAY | MONDAY | TUESDAY | WEDNESDAY | THURSDAY | FRIDAY | SATURDAY |
| | | | 1 | 2 | 3 | 4 |
| 5 | 6 | 7 | 8 | 9 | 10 | 11 |
| 12 | FINAL BOOK REPORT DUE ☆ (13) | 14 | 15 | 16 | 17 | 18 |
| 19 | 20 | 21 | 22 | 23 | 24 | 25 |
| 26 | 27 | 28 | 29 | 30 | 31 | |

2. **Divide the assignment into parts, and determine separate due dates.** Either through class discussion or teacher decision, break the assignment into small steps for students to complete. Ask students to count the total days they have to complete the assignment, then decide the amount of days to allocate for each step. It may be helpful to have students determine which steps are most time consuming, allocating those time periods first. For example, if students have six weeks to complete a book report and allocate three weeks to read the book and two weeks to write the first draft, there is one week left for choosing the book and writing the final draft.

3. **Have students count backward and mark due dates on their calendars.** Once time periods have been determined, have students count back from the final due date to assign deadline dates. Use an overhead projector and transparencies to show students how to mark these dates on their calendars. For example, if the final draft is due December 13th, students count back five days to assign December 8th as the day to begin the final draft, count back two more weeks to designate November 24th as the date to start the first draft, and so on, until all due dates are assigned.

4. **Determine daily tasks and write them on the calendar.** Have students brainstorm a list of tasks to complete for each step of the assignment, then determine which ones to perform each day. Ask students to write daily responsibilities on their calendars. For example, if a student chooses a 180-page book and there are three weeks allocated to read it, he or she would need to read twelve pages per weekday to meet the deadline. The student then writes and circles *12 pages* on each weekday up to the deadline date. As each day's assignment is complete, students can cross it off.

5. **Monitor and encourage student progress.** Have students keep backward-planning schedules in their homework folders so parents can check due dates and monitor progress. Have students choose partners to encourage progress. Acknowledge student effort throughout the process and reward students when they reach their goals.

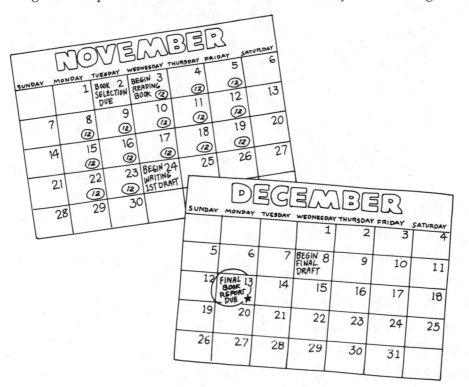

## Helping Students Complete Assignments On Time

- Include time-awareness activities in your classroom. Have students change calendar days, mark special events, and read the time before and after lessons. Verbalize the relationship of these tools to responsibility. For example, *The calendar helps us remember a scheduled event and the clock helps us be on time.*

- Post the day's events each morning. Discuss how time is allocated, and work together to keep on schedule.

- Give time warnings when an assignment is about to be collected. Write the time remaining on the chalkboard as a visual reminder.

- Challenge older students to complete assignments within a specified time frame (e.g., ten minutes to solve math problems). Repeat "time challenges" every week so students can compare their progress.

## Today's Schedule

9:00 READING
10:00 SPELLING
10:40 WRITING

| Sunday | Monday | Tuesday | Wednesday | Thursday | Friday | Saturday |
| Sun. | Mon. | Tues. | Wed. | Thurs. | Fri. | Sat. |
|---|---|---|---|---|---|---|
|  |  | 1 | 2 | 3 | 4 | 5 |
| 6 | 7 | 8 | 9 |  |  |  |
|  |  |  |  |  |  |  |
|  |  |  |  |  |  |  |
|  |  |  |  |  |  |  |

## Time-Awareness Games and Activities

**Time Passage.** Students estimate how much time has passed since they began an assignment. Those who are within five minutes of the actual time receive a reward.

**Minute Report.** Students have one minute to tell about a favorite book, including the author and favorite parts. Classmates guess the book's title based on the description.

**Book Pass.** Students sit in a circle, look at a book for thirty seconds, then pass it to the next person. After the book is passed around the circle, students share what they've learned.

**Three-Minute Cleanup.** Students have three minutes to clean up work areas. When the signal is given, they return to their seats. Those who finish in the allotted time receive a reward (e.g., dismissed for recess a minute early).

**Friday Free Time.** At the beginning of each week, tell students they have fifteen minutes of "free time" on Friday. Students earn extra minutes by being responsible and completing assignments on time. Conversely, they lose minutes when time is wasted.

**Just-a-Minute Log.** Student pairs estimate, then time the number of repetitive actions partners can complete in one minute, such as bouncing a ball, jumping rope, or solving math facts.

# Designing a Personal Discipline System

**Responsible behavior must be explicitly taught and modeled to children.**
Although parents have the largest influence, teachers should also guide and encourage character development in their students. Set the foundation for responsible behavior within the first weeks of school by implementing a personally designed system of discipline to help students self-monitor and correct their behavior. Use positive intervention techniques such as role modeling, interactive games, and incentive systems to encourage and support positive performance in your students.

## Setting the Stage for Responsible Behavior

### Step 1—Determine the Behaviors You Want to See

- Decide how you would like students to behave with during instruction and independent work periods. Consider both academic and social behavior.

- Think of typical situations that arise in your classroom and how you would like students to behave. Visualizing the ideal classroom clarifies expectations.

- List specific desirable behaviors as goals for your responsibility-training program.

### Step 2—Plan How to Teach and Encourage Desired Behavior

- Do not assume students know how to behave properly in all situations. Many need to be taught the difference between appropriate and inappropriate behavior.

- Teach lessons on how to follow directions, the difference between "reporting" and "tattling," how to stay on-task, and what to do when finished with their work.

- Conduct weekly problem-solving sessions to discuss current behavior issues, and brainstorm possible solutions.

### Step 3—Develop Ways to Keep Appropriate Behavior Reoccurring

- Many times, affirmation is all it takes to motivate students to behave. Knowing someone is aware of their efforts can be incredibly encouraging to students.

- Model genuine appreciation and respect when students behave appropriately. A simple "thank you" may have amazing results.

- Use positive incentive plans (see *Success with Incentive Systems*, pages 33–34) to encourage appropriate behavior throughout the school year. Reward direction, not perfection.

### Step 4—Anticipate What You Will Do When Inappropriate Behavior Occurs

- Positive, creative interventions are the first line of defense. For example, students often self-correct inappropriate behavior when they realize their actions are being documented.

- If students do not respond properly, determine fair and appropriate consequences such as time-out from favorite activities, or loss of classroom privileges. Involve parents if misbehavior escalates.

- Develop step-by-step systems to deal with persistant inappropriate behavior (avoiding work, stealing, cheating, name-calling), giving students reasonable choices and nurturing self-respect.

- Remember that your goal is to correct behavior, not undermine a child's self-esteem—keep calm and respectful, and always evaluate each situation independently.

### Step 5—Communicate Your Program to Students, Parents, and Administrators

- The first week of school, send parents a letter in which you clearly explain your classroom standards and expectations. Describe positive reinforcements students will receive when they follow the rules and procedures.

- Meet with parents within the first month to discuss classroom procedures. Share a variety of creative interventions that have worked for you in the past. Most parents support a discipline system that is fair and consistent.

- Let them know the importance of their support and partnership in educating their children, and encourage continued communication.

## Games and Activities that Teach Responsible Behavior

**Simon Says.** Have students practice how to watch, listen for, and follow directions by playing a light-hearted game of Simon Says. For example, reinforce the importance of student eye contact when you are speaking. Stand to the right of the classroom and have students look in your direction. Say, *Simon says, look to your right.* Move to other areas of the room and repeat the process. Omit *Simon says* from the directions (e.g., *Look at your desktop*) to catch students looking in the wrong direction. Use the opportunity to discuss the importance of looking at someone when he or she is speaking. End the activity by having students write what they learned in journals (e.g., *Simon says, write the important lesson you learned from this activity*). Repeat the process with other behaviors.

**Puppet Praise.** Puppets are a fun way to demonstrate and reinforce appropriate and inappropriate behavior. Use puppets to praise young students who respond quickly and accurately to instruction. Have older students make their own puppets and produce a puppet show teaching younger students about good behavior.

**1, 2, 3 . . . Go!** Use hand signals and verbal cues to help students follow three-part directions. First, have students listen to directions such as *Raise your hand, pat your head, and return your hand to your lap.* Tell students not to respond until they hear you say, *Go.* Repeat the directions, holding up a finger as you state each step. For example, hold one finger up and say, *Raise your hand;* two fingers, *Pat your head;* and three fingers, *Return your hand to your lap.* Review directions a third time by holding up fingers and asking students to say each step. Once this is done, say, *Go,* and have students perform the three-step task. Repeat the process throughout the year using different three-step directions.

**The Four Magic Movers.** When students are learning to walk in lines in the hallways, hold up four fingers (the four "magic movers") to remind them what makes the line move: faces forward, mouths closed, hands at your sides, and bodies behind bodies. Compare the hallways to a crowded highway, and designate them as "no passing zones"—if you pass, you're last. When all students are cooperating with the four magic movers, the line moves; when they aren't, the line stops. With consistent use and practice of this system, your students will soon learn the "rules of the road."

**The Whispering Game.** Explain the importance of whispering in various situations in and out of the classroom. Model how to whisper without straining the throat or vocal chords. Divide the class into small groups and give each group leader a card with a question or activity such as *What is your favorite food and why?* or *Make a list of adjectives.* Ask students to whisper as they complete the task. If any group breaks the "whispering barrier," points are given. The group with the lowest score wins.

**Happy Talk.** Brainstorm examples and model ways to compliment and assist others. Give students choices for handling challenging situations such as playground conflicts, cooperative-group activities, and using classroom materials. Invite young children to help make a *Happy Talk* chart of positive communication. Have older students work in cooperative groups to devise a class list of encouraging words.

## Using Humor to Correct Behavior

Students respond more readily to creativity and humor than to strict or stern commands. Do the unexpected and create a humorous atmosphere to correct and modify behavior. Consider the following light-hearted ways teachers have kept their students on-task in a safe, supportive environment.

- One primary teacher suddenly began to whisper when she realized her students weren't giving her complete attention. Students were caught off-guard not hearing the teacher's voice, looked up, and leaned forward to hear what was being said. The teacher caught their attention without upset or disruption, and the students appreciated and responded to the humor of the situation.

- A very tall math teacher looming 6' 4" into the stratosphere began talking to the wall when he realized no one was listening. The sight was irresistibly funny—everyone had a good laugh and attention was pleasantly reestablished.

- One preschool teacher used puppets to give directions, make announcements, and regain attention. Sometimes she would use a puppet to correct behavior, having the puppet act angry and upset over behavior while she defended the students' actions. Students would interact with the puppet, discussing ways to correct and modify their behavior so everyone was happy.

## Success with Incentive Systems

**Knights of the Round Table.** Give each student a black shield upon which to place stickers earned for responsible behavior such as following rules, returning homework, or being kind to others. The stickers themselves provide incentive for positive, responsible behavior.

**Classroom Banking System.** Reward students for responsible behavior with paper money, tokens, or stamps for stamp books. They may use their "money" to buy privileges (free time, homework pass, taking the class pet home). Or, have an auction at the end of the quarter—invite students to contribute small items, and bid with their earned money.

**The "Right Choice" Club.** Students become part of the club when they make a responsible choice about social interactions or study habits. They earn and accumulate time for an approved activity such as free reading, computers, and games. Discuss behavior that may keep students out of the club (e.g., talking in class inappropriately, not being on task in learning centers, tardiness), and suggest better actions to take in the future. Not every student will make it into the club at first. Those who do will feel proud of their accomplishments; those left out will be eager to earn their way in.

RIGHT CHOICE
C · L · U · B
Susie          Amy
Tommy        Trevor
Tanya

**Table Points.** Divide students into cooperative groups and reward points each time all members of the group are on task. When a group earns 25 points, they receive a reward such as free time, homework passes, or stickers.

**Marbles in a Jar.** The class earns a marble when everyone follows the rules. At the beginning of the year, reward students often so they experience the incentive quickly and are motivated to continue. As the year progresses, increase standards and make it more challenging to win marbles. Reward the class with a special treat when the jar is full or when marbles have reached a designated mark.

## Discussing and Resolving Problems with Students

- Keep the atmosphere "safe." Make every effort to remain patient and calm.

- Be supportive and constructive in your actions. Listen objectively and choose consequences that are fair and appropriate.

- Avoid using sarcasm. Children often misunderstand and take words literally.

- Be aware of peer influences. Many students will turn disagreements into power struggles to "save face." If possible, address serious conflicts in private, giving both you and the student time to regain composure.

- Acknowledge the fact that you cannot make students do anything against their will. (You just *hope* they will choose to do the "right thing.")

- Use more severe consequences (e.g., sending a student to the principal's office) only after milder consequences have failed. More serious repercussions are necessary when inappropriate behavior is repetitive or when it undermines your authority.

- Realize that students may be reacting to pressures and stress unrelated to school. Ask them about life outside of school, focusing on unexpected events or changes in the regular daily routine. If necessary, talk to parents to learn more about any outside pressures.

# Parent Interactions

**The initial impression you make with parents can set the tone for the entire school year.** Always keep the lines of communication open. A good way to start is to phone parents at the beginning of the school year. Introduce yourself, officially welcome them to your class, and answer any questions or concerns they may have. Continue to encourage two-way correspondence through phone calls, letters, conferences, and home visits. Contact parents frequently during the first trimester, then taper off as trust is developed and student performance is established. Remember to call or write parents about good news, not just when there is a problem or concern.

Use Communication Logs (reproducible, page 122) to keep track of all parent contacts, not only for your own personal reference, but for school administrators to examine when needed. Store log sheets in a binder that includes tabs labeled with student numbers (see *Personal Numbering System*, page 91), a class list containing student names and corresponding numbers for quick reference, and divider pockets for storing notes and letters from parents.

## Pointers for Phoning Parents

*Before* Calling Parents:

- Tell parents about the phone call in advance by sending home a letter. Communicate what will be discussed and set up a time to call. Ask them to have questions and/or concerns ready.

- Plan your part of the conversation by writing notes or questions.

- Put yourself in the parents' shoes— realize their reactions stem from concern for their child.

*During* Phone Calls to Parents:

- Relax—you are in charge. They may be more nervous than you.

- Check to see if they received the written note or letter indicating you would call.

- Verbalize reasons for calling. Be sure to use everyday language and check often for understanding.

- Be ready with positive comments about their son or daughter. Say something to assure them you know their child individually.

- Convey that you care. Always invite their questions and/or concerns.

- Listen patiently. Never get into an argument over the phone with a parent. If necessary, agree to meet later.

*After* Phone Calls to Parents:

- Study your notes. Correct or clarify comments you may not understand if read at a later date. Add information you inadvertently left out.

- Jot down private perceptions or questions that occurred to you after you hung up the phone.

- Follow up phone calls with a quick letter to notify parents of any progress.

## Written Communication to Parents

● Use Homework Assignment Sheets (reproducible, page 123) to encourage parents to monitor student work. Have parents write their initials by listed assignments completed each night. Use the same sheet throughout the week to communicate progress.

● Send corrected work home regularly—every day or every week depending on the age of your students. Save time by having students organize work themselves, by subject matter or date. Include a return sign-off slip with space for comments to make certain work packets have been received and reviewed by parents.

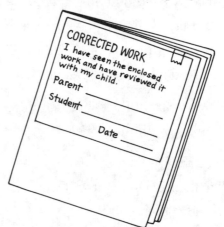

● Send home monthly newsletters that outline major goals, list skills and concepts being taught, and indicate specific work for parents to look for. Newsletters develop students' writing skills in a "real-life" setting, enable students to share their work with others, and keep parents informed of classroom happenings. Invite different student groups to be in charge of the newsletter each month. If you do not have a computer, create newsletters using handwritten work and a copy machine—glue articles on butcher paper and use a copy machine to shrink work to 8½" x 11" (21 cm x 27.5 cm).

● At least once a month, send home a positive note for each student. Keep a card file listing names, addresses, phone and fax numbers, and e-mail information for each student. Before school, pull out two cards and place them on your desk to remind you which students receive letters that day. Use stick-on notes to help you remember important information to include. Diffuse any student anxiety by sharing notes with students in private before sending them home to parents.

● Make monthly memo booklets for students to take home and share with parents. For each child, bind together nine flat paper sacks (i.e., stationery card bags), one for each month of the school year. At the beginning of each month, invite students to decorate the outside of a sack with seasonal illustrations. Place corrected papers inside the sack throughout the month. At the end of each month, send the booklet home, asking students to return it the next day. Store booklets in student portfolios, and send them home permanently at the end of the school year.

## Sharing Student Success through Portfolios

Create individual portfolios that contain samples of each student's work (papers, audio-tapes, special assignments) collected throughout the year. These folders or storage boxes are valuable "time lines," showing both teacher and parents a student's progress over time. Keep portfolios at school until the end of the year. Invite parents to visit the class-room and view collected samples.

Encourage students to actively participate in the learning process by self-selecting and assessing portfolio samples (see Self-Evaluation Log reproducible, page 124). Once a week, hold a "portfolio party," and invite students to choose which completed assign-ments to add to their portfolios. Ask them to review past portfolio entries, then decide on one or two new samples to add to their collections. (Be certain all entries are dated and evaluated before being placed in the file.) Collect work from one subject area to start, then expand into other curriculum areas. Have students self-assess their work—explain why the piece was selected, what they like best about it, what they learned from doing the assignment, and what they would do differently. At least once per quarter, conduct individual or small-group conferences to discuss portfolio selections. Decide together which items should remain in the portfolio and which items to send home. This "weed-ing out" process will help you manage portfolios more easily as well as provide immediate feedback to parents.

## Helping Students Communicate Effectively to Parents

When parents ask their children, *What did you learn at school today?*, the most common reply is, *Nothing*. Alleviate this communication problem by having students keep daily journals. Invite students to reflect on the day's events through writing, discussion, and role-playing. Allocate 30 minutes to begin with, then less time as writing skills improve and the need for role-playing decreases.

- Ask students, *What did you learn in school today?*, then write responses on the chalkboard.

- Have each student choose one or two items from the list to write about in his or her journal. Be certain students date each entry.

- Ask each student to read the day's entry silently or to a partner. Invite several volunteers to read their comments aloud.

- Have students practice telling their parents what they did at school that day. Choose four or five students to role-play the conversation with you acting as parent.

- The next day, invite students to share conversations they had with their parents.

- Keep journals at school until the end of the year. Remember, the goal is to encourage oral communication.

## Welcoming Visitors

We often become so busy that we fail to acknowledge the presence of a guest in the room. Whether a visit is planned or spontaneous, greet the guest warmly by making eye contact and saying hello. Even if a parent comes to your classroom every Wednesday, make him or her feel welcome.

Clarify to students how to behave when guests are in the classroom. Have them practice proper guest etiquette—greeting a guest at the door, welcoming the guest to the classroom, making introductions, and showing him or her where to sit. Remind students that yelling hello across the room is inappropriate—a smile or wave can accomplish the same greeting. There may be times when student enthusiasm over a special guest disrupts the lesson. In these situations, be flexible and understanding.

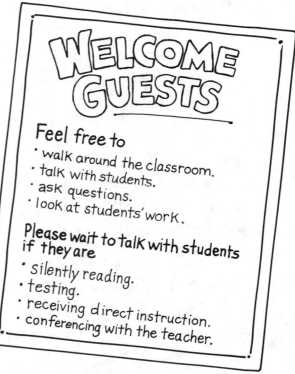

Take the first step and invite parents and administrators to visit the classroom at special times throughout the year. They will appreciate the opportunity to visit and will feel warmly welcomed by the invitation. Be sure guests feel at ease by setting aside a comfortable place to sit and offering a secure place to store coats and other personal belongings. Help visitors "fit in" by posting your classroom procedures and clarifying proper protocol. Briefly stop lessons and have students share current classroom happenings. Have extra copies of your weekly newsletter available for guests to read and enjoy.

At times, the number of university observers, community volunteers, or resource personnel who interrupt your class may be overwhelming. Remember, you do not have to say yes to everyone. For example, train a student teacher every other year instead of every year, have parent volunteers help Monday through Thursday only, or set aside Wednesdays only for guests.

# Working with Paraprofessionals

**Paraprofessionals (paid assistants and volunteer helpers) need to feel a sense of belonging, purpose, and pride in their jobs.** Relay the importance of their contributions and create a successful partnership by including them in decisions, clearly outlining responsibilities, providing personal work space, and offering supportive feedback.

- Give paid assistants their own place in the classroom, including adult furniture. Invite them to personalize their space, legitimizing their position and role in the classroom.

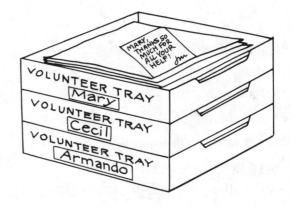

- For volunteers, designate personal holding trays (stackable plastic trays) for assignments and written correspondence to make them feel welcome and part of the classroom routine.

- Give paraprofessionals a complete list of job options from which to choose. Invite them to rank their choices from "most preferred" to "least preferred." Keep a copy of the ranked list and try to honor as many preferences as possible.

- Help paraprofessionals set and achieve professional goals. Take time each month—before school starts, during lunch, or after school—to discuss and decide on goals. For example, if a paraprofessional has trouble staying on schedule, post visual reminders. Visual reminders such as stick-on notes can also establish good habits.

- Develop job cards that outline ongoing tasks. On each card, write explicit directions and where materials are located. Color and laminate cards, placing them in a file box near volunteers' holding trays. After choosing a specific activity, pull out the corresponding job card, add a stick-on note identifying students to include, and place it in the volunteer's holding tray.

- Be supportive and communicative with paraprofessionals. Give frequent positive feedback and offer constructive suggestions for improvement.

- Show consideration and respect. Use various nonverbal cues during lesson times to indicate needs or concerns—pointing to your ear to indicate high noise level, thumbs up to indicate approval or success, stick-on notes to communicate important messages.

# People Management Review

## Did you:

 establish a trusting and caring classroom environment through positive verbal and nonverbal behavior?

 make all students feel welcome and valued in your classroom by referring to them by name and taking time to learn about their lives outside of the classroom?

 help students feel like part of the classroom community by enlisting their help with classroom procedures and accommodating individual learning styles?

 systematically monitor student progress, explicitly stating your expectations, giving specific praise for progress, and offering assistance when needed?

✓ encourage students to take charge of their own learning by helping them set goals, make responsible choices, monitor their time, and plan ahead?

✓ clarify expectations and reinforce appropriate student behavior through positive intervention techniques such as verbal feedback, activities and games, and incentive plans?

✓ develop a positive partnership with parents by keeping them well informed of their children's progress through regular written and verbal correspondence?

✓ help visitors feel welcome in your classroom by greeting them warmly, clarifying the classroom routine, and sharing current happenings?

✓ show appreciation and respect toward paraprofessionals—inviting them to personalize their work space, including them in decisions, giving supportive and corrective feedback, and developing a friendly rapport?

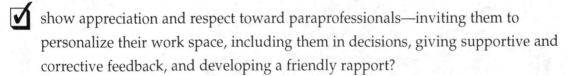

*" Coming together is a beginning;*
*Keeping together is progress;*
*Working together is success. "*
—*Henry Ford*

# SPACE MANAGEMENT

Classroom space is a finite resource, yet "magically" expands through creativity and imagination. Modern classroom instruction fluctuates between whole-class experiences, small teacher-facilitated groups, independent teams of collaborating students, and the individual learner. Students need space for mobility, hands-on learning, exploration and discovery, and treasured moments of reflection. Maximizing and creatively managing space enables you to efficiently establish classroom routines within your teaching philosophy and to "open up" larger spaces of learning.

## In this chapter, you will

- assess your use of classroom space.

- gain practical tips for classroom furniture arrangement.

- determine ways to organize your personal work area.

- learn to create fun and practical bulletin-board displays.

- discover innovative uses of wall, floor, and air space.

> " A strong, successful man is not the victim of his environment. He creates favorable conditions. His own inherent force and energy compel things to turn out as he desires."
> —Orison Swett Marden

# Setting Up the Classroom

**Before deciding on your room arrangement, measure the amount of floor space available and compare it to the space you need for classroom furniture and large equipment (desks, file cabinets, throw rugs, overhead projectors, computers).** Based on the amount of space needed, allocate portions of the room to each item. To avoid extra moving and lifting, use a tape measure to determine whether large items will fit in certain classroom locations.

Consider student mobility and visibility when arranging furniture in your classroom. Be sure to provide

- easy access to and from desk areas and resource centers.

- enough space for students to move between and around all furniture, especially near busy areas such as the pencil sharpener, doorways, supply cabinets, and your work area.

- open pathways so that permanent furniture does not block movement of mobile equipment (computers, TV monitors, overhead projectors).

- clear visual pathways from all areas of the classroom. Avoid using tall cabinets or displays that interfere with your ability to monitor students.

- easy viewing of maps, overhead-projector screen, and TV monitor.

As you decide how to best use your floor space, also consider the "flexibility" of your furniture—whether it can be easily moved or used for other purposes. Using furniture that is mobile or multi-functional offers more flexibility and gives you more space to work.

## Classroom Space Inventory

Use the following inventory to assess your current use of classroom space. Place a check by each statement that describes your learning environment, and add any additional statements about your classroom at the end of the list.

### Use of Flexible Furniture

❏ Tables, chairs, and desks can be easily moved or stacked.

❏ Learning centers fold and move for easy storage.

❏ Some cupboards are on wheels.

❏ Crates and other handy containers are used for short-term units, "check-out" materials, and consumable supplies.

### Permanent Resource Areas

❏ Classroom library

❏ Writing center

❏ Science lab

❏ Math center

❏ Others _____

### High Traffic Areas

❏ Easy access to pencil sharpeners and trash cans.

❏ Easy mobility through doorways and between desks.

❏ Sufficient space around supply areas and bookshelves.

❏ Adequate space to move among group work areas.

### Instructional Presentations and Displays

❏ Students easily see chalkboards, overhead-projector screen, and TV monitor.

❏ Flannel boards or story boards are clearly visible.

❏ All students see pull-down maps.

### Monitoring Students

❏ Students can be seen at all times.

❏ Low cabinets separate areas.

❏ Desk arrangement enables close proximity to students.

❏ Students are close to instructional areas for good eye contact.

### Classroom Environment and Learning Modalities

❏ Supports auditory (hearing) learning.

❏ Supports visual (seeing) learning.

❏ Supports kinesthetic (moving) learning.

❏ Supports tactile (touching) learning.

### Room Arrangement and Learning Styles

❏ Accommodates individualized learning.

❏ Accommodates collaborative learning.

❏ Accommodates concrete learning.

❏ Accommodates abstract learning.

❏ Accommodates sequential learning.

### Office in the Classroom

❏ A functional and comfortable place to work.

❏ Desktop is clear of all distractions.

❏ Files are conveniently located close to my desk.

❏ Planning guides and textbooks are easily accessible.

❏ Monthly wall calendars are posted close by for long-term planning.

## Meaningful Use of Bulletin Boards

❏ Display a variety of student work.

❏ Communicate important information in simple terms.

❏ Graphically teach crucial concepts using pictures and charts.

❏ Cleverly "store" student materials.

❏ Provide teaching/learning resource areas.

## Inviting and Motivating Environment

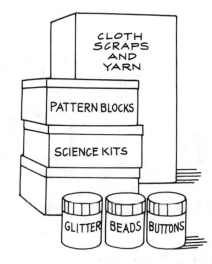

❏ Clean and orderly room.

❏ Exhibits a variety of colorful and exciting displays.

❏ Displays student work everywhere.

❏ Displays samples of decision-making.

❏ Classroom furniture appropriate for the students.

❏ Containers and shelves are labeled.

❏ Materials for a variety of learning opportunities are available.

❏ Friendly, helpful, and encouraging climate.

❏ Conducive to both formal study and informal interactions.

❏ Stimulating ambiance but not overly distracting.

❏ Positive, safe, and task-oriented atmosphere.

## Other Statements Describing Your Use of Classroom Space

_____

_____

_____

_____

_____

# Arranging Classroom Furniture

**The way you arrange classroom furniture depends on your teaching style and student needs.** Use the following sample floor plans in combination with suggested student-desk arrangements (see pages 52–56) to set up your classroom.

## Floor Plan A

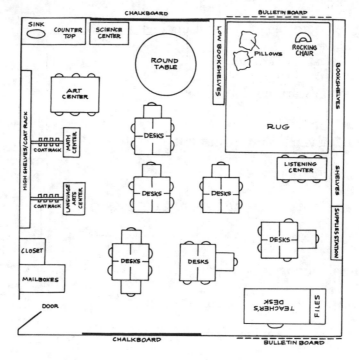

## Major Features

- Student desks arranged in clusters to open up the classroom.

- Desk clusters can also be used for additional learning centers or cooperative-group activities.

- Permanent language arts, math, art, and science centers are situated next to each other for easier rotation.

- The art and science centers are placed close to the sink for easy project preparation and cleanup.

- The listening center is situated in a quiet area of the classroom.

- The library includes pillows and a rocking chair to offer comfort while reading, and to accommodate different learning modalities.

- The teacher's desk is easily accessible, out of major traffic areas, and permits the teacher to easily monitor all areas of the classroom while conducting one-to-one conferences.

- Bookshelves and storage cabinets are placed along the edges of the classroom to allow easy access and free up more floor space.

# Floor Plan B

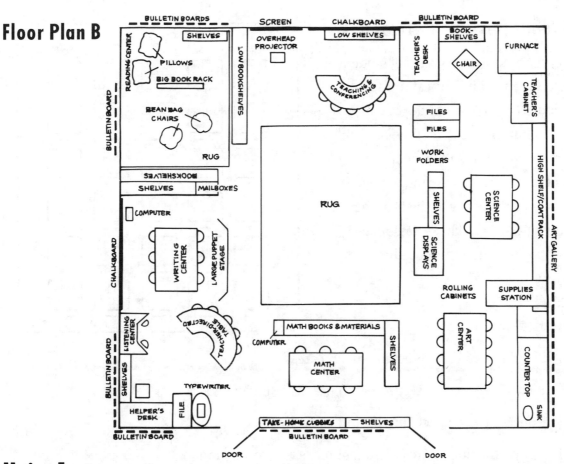

## Major Features

- The rug area dominates the classroom's central space. It can be used for instruction, class meetings, hands-on projects, and storytelling circles.

- No assigned seating—whole-class instruction is conducted with students sitting on a rug, using individual lap boards. For longer lessons, tables are moved to the rug area.

- Learning centers are prominent. They may be used to encourage self-selection during independent, partner, and small-group explorations. They may also be used by parent volunteers for special small-group lessons.

- Materials needed for different subjects are stored by corresponding learning centers for easier access and organization.

- Two teaching tables are included for small-group and personalized conferences. They are situated at opposite ends of the classroom so the teacher and instructional assistant may work simultaneously without distracting each other.

- The teacher's personal work space forms an "office area" with all teaching materials within easy reach, and includes an extra chair for private student-teacher conferences.

## Student Desks—Vertical Rows

This configuration consists of student desks arranged in vertical rows, one desk directly in back of the other. Research indicates that "time on-task" is improved and student achievement is enhanced with this arrangement. It is also very effective at the beginning of the year when whole-class focus is essential as you teach procedures and routines.

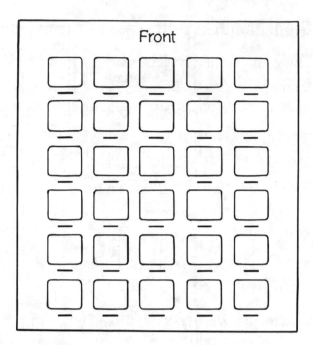

### Benefits

- All students can see direct instruction areas.

- Student "territory" is secure—each has his or her own desk.

- Interfering eye contact among students is limited.

- Fewer distractions increase student focus and concentration.

- Individual effort is maximized.

### Disadvantages

- Monitoring is more difficult—it's harder to get close to students.

- Effective eye contact is only in the front of the room.

- Student interaction is limited—they only see backs of heads.

- Students in back of the room feel more isolated.

### Ways to Overcome Disadvantages

- Move up and down the rows for eye contact and proximity.

- Pull two rows together to increase student interaction and make room for resource areas near the edges of the classroom.

- Rotate students to the front every week or month.

## Student Desks—Horseshoe Formation

This configuration consists of desks arranged in a semi-circle, with groups of three aligned vertically. This arrangement is very effective for viewing performances, group presentations, solo reports, and watching films and videos.

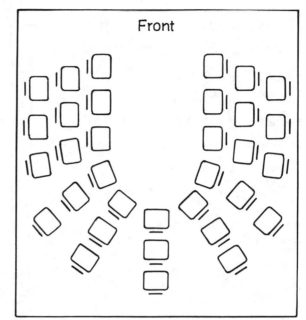

### Benefits

- All students can see direct instruction areas.

- Student "territory" is secure—each has his or her own desk.

- Effective eye contact can be maintained by the teacher.

- Teams of three can quickly form for collaboration.

- Students see many more faces and feel less isolated.

- Proximity is easily accomplished through the wide center walkway.

### Disadvantages

- Students seeing many faces encourages more interfering behavior and distractions.

- Students at the outside edges of the desk formation tend to feel more isolated.

### Ways to Overcome Disadvantages

- Set high standards for listening.

- Rotate students every week or month.

- Divide the horseshoe into three distinct sections with some friendly competition among the three teams to create positive peer pressure.

## Student Desks—Triad Teams

This configuration consists of triad desk teams arranged in horizontal rows. Studies show that clusters of three evoke a stronger group mentality than other numerical combinations. Students in each triad face inward, creating an ideal environment for team "spirit," with reduced chances of exclusion.

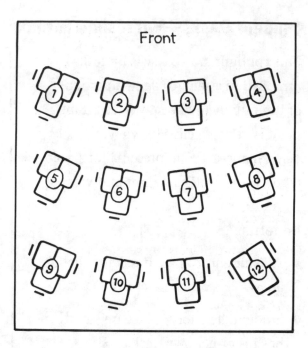

### Benefits

- All students can see direct instruction areas.

- Teacher can easily alternate between direct instruction and team practice.

- Teams of six form easily for more complex group work.

- Teacher proximity and eye contact takes place easily.

### Disadvantages

- Physical closeness of teams may be distracting.

- Occasionally, there is the "odd person out" syndrome.

- Students may be tempted to copy from other triad members.

- One student may carry a disproportionate load.

- A student's low performance may be masked by other members of the triad.

### Ways to Overcome Disadvantages

- Keep a quick, energetic pace when alternating between direct instruction and team practice.

- Include team-building activities.

- Use enthusiasm and attention-getting techniques during direct instruction.

- Make your physical presence known by monitoring each triad. Your presence alone will encourage critical thinking and on-task behavior.

## Student Desks—Groups of Four

Student desks are arranged in groups of four with students facing inward. Quads are angled to optimize front viewing.

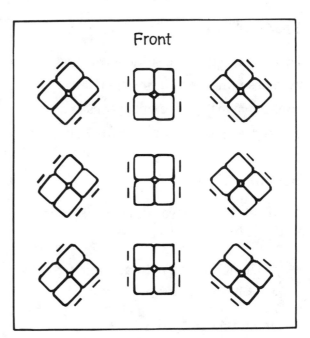

Front

### Benefits

- Teamwork and direct instruction can alternate quickly.

- Collaborative learning and closeness is a natural product.

- Teams of two can easily form within each group, providing partnering advantages.

- Teacher proximity and eye contact takes place easily.

- Offers the space advantage of a large table while still providing individual territories.

### Disadvantages

- Student interaction at the wrong time is almost inevitable.

- The larger the group, the greater the chances of off-task behavior.

- All groups of even numbers have a greater potential to form exclusive subgroups, sometimes in unfriendly competition.

### Ways to Overcome Disadvantages

- Use short mini-lessons and lots of collaborative work.

- Teach students cooperative-learning strategies and social skills necessary for successful group work.

- Use inclusion exercises for team building.

- Reconfigure the teams and frequently change seating for greater effectiveness.

## Student Tables

In this configuration, students are seated at tables rather than individual desks. Tables may be of different shapes and sizes. They are angled to optimize front viewing.

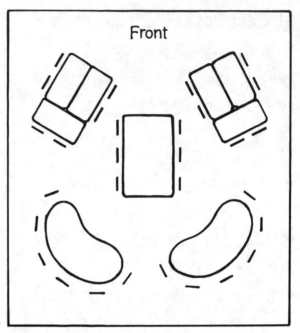

### Benefits

- All students can see direct instruction areas.

- Collaboration is a natural outgrowth— teams of two and three.

- Provides large work surfaces.

- Proximity and eye contact are easily maintained.

- Friendly competition between tables is great motivation.

### Disadvantages

- Student territory is less defined.

- Most tables provide no space for student materials.

- Management issues arise around personal property.

- Closeness of students around a table can be distracting, and detecting the key culprit more difficult.

### Ways to Overcome Disadvantages

- Provide cubbies elsewhere for personal items, and shelves for textbooks.

- Provide baskets of group supplies at each table (pencils, paper, rulers) with specific guidelines for their use.

- Teach cooperative-learning strategies, including team-building activities for inclusion.

- Reconfigure groups as needed. Slight changes can alter group dynamics dramatically.

- Rotate whole groups to new tables so students view the teacher and classroom from a fresh viewpoint.

## Flexible Furniture Features

- Use fold-up, learning-center displays placed on student desks, resource tables, or the floor instead of permanent learning-center stations.

- Leave enough space alongside classroom walls to stack student desks and chairs, freeing up floor space for storytelling, discussion circles, and hands-on explorations.

- Have students play games or complete projects on portable, fold-up card tables outside the classroom door. Outdoor activities may be used to expand available work space as well as offer special rewards to those who finish work early.

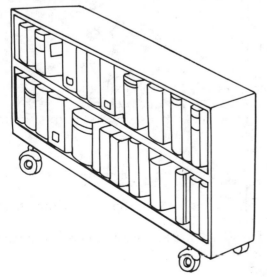

- Use a roll-away book cart rather than a stationary bookcase for your class library. Use rolling carts for any center activity that could be accommodated outside, such as a construction set, sink-and-float activities, or papier-mâché art. Wheel carts outside for the day and bring them back inside when school is over.

- Allow one or two responsible students to work at your desk during class time. Not only will this provide additional desk space, students will feel special and important.

- Many schools have unused space in "hidden," out-of-the-way places. Hunt around— occasionally there's a closet or part of the classroom not being used to its fullest potential. Invite parent volunteers to fix up the area for different purposes such as a cooking station, publishing center, or science lab. When areas are available *outside* your classroom, have a paraprofessional or parent take small groups of students to the locations, thus expanding the amount of work space and reducing the noise level in the classroom.

- Team with another teacher to expand the amount of space your students can enjoy. For example, if each teacher has three learning centers, students may experience six centers as they rotate through both classrooms.

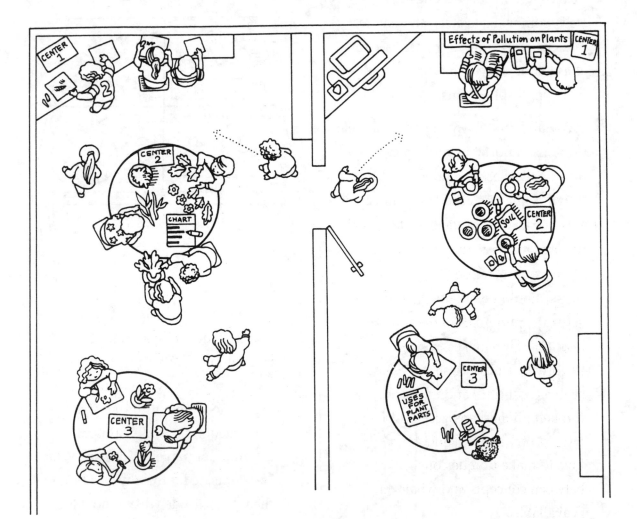

# Accommodating Learning Modalities

**Provide a learning environment that accommodates all modalities—audio (hearing), visual (seeing), kinesthetic (moving), and tactile (touching).** Consider these suggestions as you arrange your classroom to meet student needs.

- Designate quiet work areas for students who are easily distracted, and discussion tables for those who need to verbalize ideas before starting written work.

- Provide open floor space with large pillows, bean bags, and lap desks for students who need to spread out while reading, playing games, or completing projects.

- Place students with low attention spans away from the classroom door, windows, class pets, or high-traffic areas.

- Situate learning centers away from the class library or quiet work areas to keep all students on-task.

- Reserve an area of the classroom for a variety of resources from which students can choose. Although most items should be organized into small, separate, portable storage containers, also offer large boxes, trunks, or bags filled with an assortment of items such as costumes and machine parts (broken phones, answering machines, tape recorders, etc.). Some students love to make unique connections between concepts and whatever is available.

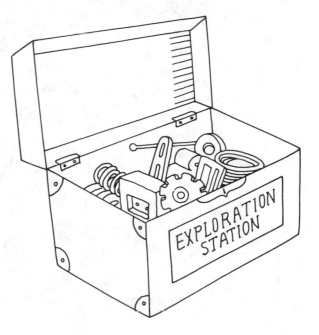

- Reserve space for a permanent listening center. Auditory learners prefer listening to a recording of a book rather than reading it. Increase learning by encouraging students to follow along in the book as they listen to the tape.

- Set aside space for picture books, picture files, filmstrips, videos, and illustrated dictionaries for visual learners. They remember concepts better if they have pictures/illustrations along with words.

- Reserve space for big books, construction activities, and large game boards for kinesthetic learners. Include bowls or flat, plastic containers filled with clay or sand so younger tactile learners can mold clay letters or use their fingers to draw letters in sand.

# Establishing Personal Work Space

**It is crucial to have a quiet place to plan with all the needed resources and information close at hand.** Plan your "office in the classroom" carefully—space is valuable and every bit should be used to enhance student learning.

## Furniture Arrangement

Be sure to select a corner of your classroom away from the door. Angle the desk so you can see students from where you sit. This enables you to scan and monitor the class as you conduct personal conferences with students. Place a file cabinet near your desk to organize all papers involved with teaching, assessing, planning, evaluating, and implementing (see *Paperwork Management,* pages 97–110). Use a low bookshelf behind your desk to store frequently-used curriculum guides, teacher's editions of textbooks, student folders, and other needed resources. Arrange furniture so there is enough open space for mobility, and place an extra chair in the vicinity for students or parents to use during conferencing.

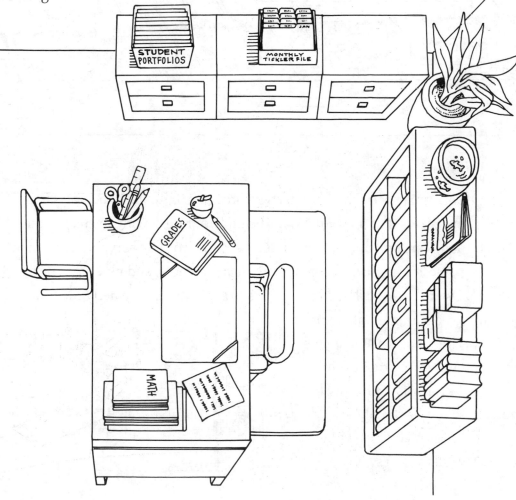

## Desk Storage

Keep the inside of your desk well-stocked and organized with supplies. Note items you use as you work in your "office." Over time, you can collect all the resources and tools you need to do your job effectively. As you store items in your desk, consider what you want at your fingertips. The middle desk drawer typically contains various pens, pencils (regular and colored), rulers, rubber stamps (for student papers), notepads, and stick-on notes of various sizes and colors. Use shallow desk drawers to hold daily forms—hall passes, small rewards, lunch-count forms, reminder notes for absentees, and stationery. Place reusable hanging folders in the bottom desk drawer to set up an "administrivia" file system (see *Setting Up Files*, pages 105–108).

## Environment

Make your work area special and unique with attractive organizational tools, personal mementos, and plants. Fill one of the walls behind your desk with an enlarged monthly calendar for long-term planning. Use colored pens to record important information on the calendar (e.g., red for holidays, green for parent conferences, and blue for staff-development days). Use different-colored highlighters to show the anticipated time frame for long-term projects or integrated units, filling in specific details as the unit is taught. Communicate pride in your personal and professional history by posting photographs (family and friends, past class pictures, favorite hobbies) as well as professional certificates and awards.

# Discovering "Hidden" Space

**As you set up classroom displays and centers, look for ways to use space above, between, and below classroom furniture.** There is lots of "hidden" space you can use to enhance learning in your classroom. Flat surfaces such as cabinet side panels, doors, chalkboards, and windows can be used for enrichment activities and posting work. Displays that "reach out" maximize your use of air space, freeing up wall and floor space. Consider the following suggestions to help you use every corner of available space in your classroom. (Note: If you choose to hang items directly from the ceiling, be sure you check the fire codes at your school.)

- Use windows to highlight student work by displaying transparencies of student-made stories, pictures, and/or poems. Windows can show student-painted murals, holiday scenes, seasonal changes, and symbols of a current theme. If you have too many windows, cover them with bulletin-board material.

- Use cabinet doors to display inspiring posters, enlarged writing samples, or procedural reminders (e.g., tips for making an art project, how to edit or revise writing). The inside of cabinet doors are particularly helpful for hanging pockets to hold specialized items such as calculators, dissecting kits, or games.

- Prop up Peg-Board on chalk racks to store materials such as alphabet and word cards, favorite poetry, grading keys, and handwriting models. Hang materials on Peg-Board hooks by grouping them together on a ring.

- Post information (e.g., vocabulary words, math facts, notices of upcoming events) on the inside surface of the classroom door.

- Don't forget the part of the wall touching the ceiling. Use large, colorful center signs to communicate where resource areas are located, or post enlarged time lines for students to study at leisure. This reserves more lower wall space for student-work displays.

- The sides of metal file cabinets are perfect for magnet-related activities such as making words with magnetic letters or counting with magnetic numbers. To expand your use of the magnetic surface, glue small magnets (or use peel-and-stick refrigerator magnet sheets) to the backs of word and picture cards or student photos.

- Attach wire or string horizontally across one side of the classroom to make a "clothesline" for displaying student work. Hang the string at a safe height well above students' heads. Use clothespins to clip work to the line.

- Hang fishing line vertically from the ceiling above each student's desk to display completed work. (Be certain string does not interfere with adults walking through the room.)

- Hang content-related, student-made mobiles and banners from the ceiling for decorative displays.

- Hang plants in classroom corners as part of a science unit or to create a natural, greenhouse atmosphere.

- Place a tree branch in a Styrofoam or wood base, then set it on a bookshelf or the floor to create a 3-D "tree." Invite students to decorate it by hanging items such as seasonal ornaments, poems, vocabulary definitions, and homonyms.

- If space (and your school district) permits, consider building a loft. A simple two-story wood loft can add more floor space in your classroom and provides highly desirable reading and exploration/discovery space for your students. Be sure to follow safety requirements to construct a sturdy, safe loft area.

- Create 3-D bulletin-board displays. For example, create a display entitled *Hats Off to You!* with a cardboard arm holding a hat extending out of the board. Have students drop positive notes into the hat, and on Friday afternoons, read the notes aloud and present them to the appropriate students.

# Practical Bulletin-Board Displays

**How you use classroom bulletin boards is important for creating a dynamic and productive classroom environment.** Bulletin-board displays should not only be colorful and fun, but practical and functional. Use the following ideas to help you create meaningful displays throughout the year. Save time and money by taking pictures of favorite bulletin-board displays before storing pieces for future use. Photograph the over-all view as well as close-ups to remind you of the layout, then place labeled pictures in a scrapbook. Place cutout display letters in separate resealable plastic bags—one word per bag. Clip the bags in word order to simplify posting the display at a later date. Store letters and other pieces for each display in separate, oversized file folders with titles written on the fronts for easy reference. Include notes in the folders to remind you how items were displayed.

## Individualized Bulletin Boards

Create individualized bulletin boards by dividing a large bulletin board into sections and assigning them to students. Individualized bulletin boards allow students to display self-selected work such as completed assignments or artwork.

### General Setup

Divide a large bulletin board or wall space into 12" x 18" (30 cm x 45 cm) sections using yarn or construction paper. Have students decorate and post name plates in their assigned sections. Ask students to choose new work to display once or twice a month. To stimulate awareness and discussion, have students include a criteria card listing reasons why each piece was selected.

## Advantages

- No matter what day of the school year, when an administrator or parent walks in, every child has work on display.

- Putting students in charge of their own bulletin board saves you time.

- Having each student determine his or her "personal best" for the display is an easy way to introduce self-evaluation.

- Having personal space increases students' sense of belonging.

- Students enjoy and take pride in having their own special spot to share with others.

## Display Ideas

**All About Me**—Students post and share photographs and mementos about their lives, including family, friends, pets, hobbies, and special interests.

**My Family Tree**—Students display individual family trees.

**Celebrate the Holidays**—Students decorate with handmade items appropriate to the holiday. (Encourage each student to display items unique to their racial, ethnic, or family traditions.)

**The Way I Understand It**—Students visually portray a learned concept. For example, drawing six sets of nine objects to represent 6 x 9.

**Verifying Values**—Students find a magazine picture that communicates a value such as kindness, honesty, responsibility, courage, or perseverance.

**Select-a-Sport**—Students select a sport and illustrate everything they know about it. They may write a story about the sport, list related words, draw pictures, or use magazine pictures to create a sports collage for their special spot.

**Antonym Art**—Students visually show opposites. When finished, students pair up with partners and take turns guessing which antonyms are portrayed.

**Wall Dictionaries**—Each student chooses a letter and finds all the words he or she can that begin with that letter. Words are displayed with corresponding construction-paper letters. For example, *M* to go with *mouse, money,* and *monster.*

## Bulletin Boards that Manage

Besides being decorative and educational, bulletin boards can also help you manage daily activities. You can create functional, interactive bulletin-board displays for both independent and group work.

### General Setup

Use a staple gun to attach cardboard caddies (small boxes) or laminated construction-paper pockets to a bulletin board. Decorate and use the caddies for independent, small-group, or whole-class activities filling them with supplies such as student folders, journals, and work packets.

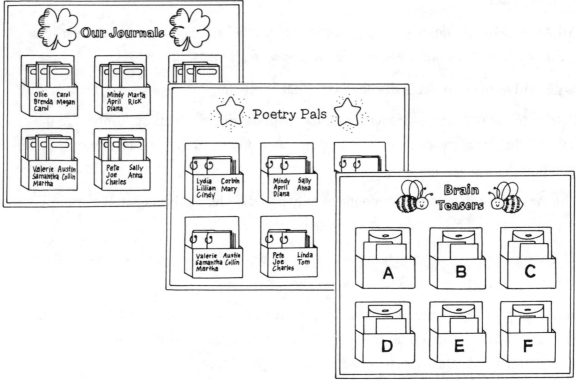

### Advantages

- The basic structure of the bulletin board never changes—only decoratives are added around the caddies/pockets to fit new themes, holidays, or seasons.

- Supplies remain in better shape than if stored inside student desks.

- Supplies are easily accessible to both students and the teacher.

- Student work can be checked or corrected in groups (one caddie/pocket at a time).

- Student work is on display for classmates, parents, and administrators to enjoy.

## Display Ideas

**Our Journals**—Each caddie holds four or five student journals, and corresponding student names or personal numbers are attached on the outside using velcro or tape. One student is designated "Keeper of the Journals." He or she is responsible for distributing and collecting journals.

**Poetry Pals**—Caddies hold favorite poems written on large index cards and held together with loose-leaf rings. Students copy their favorite poems onto the cards and add their own original compositions to share with others.

**Pen Pals**—Laminated pockets hold addresses, pictures, and descriptions of children from around the world. A world map focuses attention on the countries involved by connecting the pocket to the appropriate country with colorful yarn. Place paper, special pens, and envelopes in larger cardboard caddies.

**Practice Makes Perfect**—Teams (e.g., spelling team, multiplication team, handwriting team) are formed for students who need extra practice on a specific skill. Students select or are assigned to partners or small groups. Store flash cards or other self-checking materials in the caddies.

**Behavior Management**—Attach library pockets, with student names or numbers written on the outside, to the bulletin board. Place three different-colored cards in each pocket to indicate behavior—green in front means all is going well, yellow means a warning is in place, and red indicates disciplinary action. (Note that each day begins with a "clean slate"—all students start with a green card in their pockets.)

## Bulletin Boards that Teach

Bulletin boards may be used to teach concepts and skills such as letter-writing, graphing, problem-solving, or measurement, in the same way you might use a chart, diagram, or overhead projector. They can provide the visual support a teacher needs to clarify what is being taught by modeling examples as well as displaying practice and review activities. These bulletin boards may be posted for long periods of time and work with a wide range of grade levels.

### General Setup

When creating a teaching bulletin board, choose a concept or skill that needs to be visualized or practiced over a period of time, such as letter-writing, problem-solving, or measurement. Display a poster, map, or graph portraying the important points of the concept. Make the bulletin board using fadeless paper for backing and neutral colors for the borders because it will be up all year. Include cardboard caddies to hold needed supplies and/or place shelves under the bulletin board to store necessary materials.

### Advantages

- Important parts of the curriculum are quickly communicated to students.

- The displays may be used as centers to save space and provide "fast-finisher" activities for those who complete work early.

- The displays guide students as they learn new concepts and practice new skills.

## Display Ideas

**Opinion Graphs**—Create a large bar graph using student pictures and topic cards (e.g., favorite foods, colors, sports, or school subjects) to display student choices. Invite each child to place his or her picture on the graph to correspond with his or her preference. Keep the title permanent and change the topic to create new graph displays. Store photographs in a cardboard caddie when not on the graph.

**Writing Letters**—Create a colorful poster modeling friendly-letter format as the central focus of the display. Place a collection of names and addresses (relatives, pen pals, local companies, publishing houses, newspapers, television stations, government officials) in cardboard caddies for students to select from as they practice writing skills.

**Map Skills**—Using an overhead projector, enlarge and trace a map of your community onto a bulletin board covered with butcher paper. Have each child draw a picture of his or her home and place it around the map. Use yarn or colored string to connect each home to the correct map location. Include other important landmarks on the map to initiate discussions about the community.

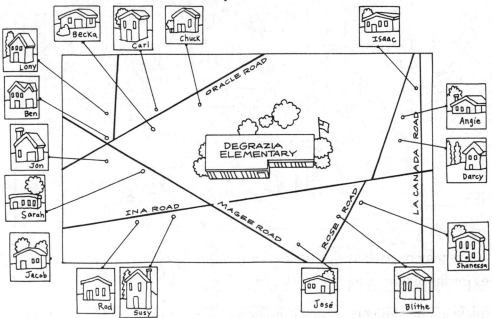

## Classroom Art Gallery

Create an art gallery in your classroom by displaying student art. Uniquely frame art selections, and have students sign their artwork just like professionals. If possible, have students study artists and illustrators, choosing projects that correlate with famous works of art. Also, select projects related to a particular theme, and increase awareness of various materials and creative methods used in the artwork.

### General Setup

Choose one or two student samples from each project to include in the art gallery. Assure students that everyone's art will hang in the gallery sometime during the year. Let them know that effort and enjoyment, not just talent or skill, will be part of the criteria for selection. If available, hang some reproductions of famous artists or book illustrators alongside student work.

If you have limited space, display one-fourth of students' work each quarter, and invite parents to view their children's art before putting up a new display. If you have ample room or choose to use an entire wall for the art gallery, art projects can accumulate all year, providing a visual record of the year's work for Open House. If you prefer, store selected pieces after each project is complete and save for an end-of-the-year display.

## Advantages

- Students who learn best spatially and tactually especially benefit from this experience.

- Classroom art galleries provide a visual record of all art projects.

- Art galleries are impressive exhibits for Open House.

- Since the art gallery develops gradually, it's an easy project to maintain.

- Self-esteem is strengthened when students see their artwork uniquely framed.

- Better self-image may develop as students see their work displayed with those of famous artists or illustrators.

- Awareness and appreciation for artists and illustrators grow as students make connections with the processes involved in producing works of art.

## Display Ideas

**Art across the Curriculum**—Include art projects tied into reading, math, social studies, science, and language arts.

**Art Time Line**—Include art projects correlating to important historical time periods.

**Multimedia Display**—Display artwork involving different mediums such as pencils, crayons, ink, cut paper, watercolors, chalk, string, colored sand, and pastels.

**High-Tech Art**—Display graphic art produced through use of computers.

**Collage Art**—Include projects illustrating different kinds of collages (cloth, paper, macaroni, leaves, miscellaneous craft objects).

**Knick-Knack Art**—Display gadget imprints in paint (string, sponge pieces, cotton balls).

**International Art**—Display art projects from different cultures, geographic regions, or ethnic groups.

# Space Management Review

## Did you:

 assess your current use of classroom space?

 arrange furniture to allow free mobility, offer a clear visual pathway, and meet student needs?

 choose a seating arrangement that fits your teaching style and meets the needs of your students?

☑ use mobile and "flexible" furniture in your classroom?

☑ set up a personalized "office" within the classroom, keeping important materials and papers within reach, using nearby walls for long-term planning, and making the area inviting to others?

☑ look for and use "hidden" surfaces and open space—windows, classroom doors, cabinet doors, chalkboards, upper wall areas, and ceilings?

☑ create fun and functional bulletin-board displays, including individualized boards, art displays, bulletin boards that manage, and displays that teach new concepts?

*" Start by doing what's necessary, then what's possible, and suddenly you are doing the impossible. "*
*—St. Francis of Assisi*

# MATERIALS MANAGEMENT

Accessibility of materials is not only essential to the serene spirit of the successful teacher, but also one of the keys to effective teaching. Organizing the classroom to meet storage requirements for a wide variety of materials is an essential, challenging, on-going task. Student materials and supplies, plus personal items, must be taken into consideration and made quickly accessible.

The following chapter provides systematic approaches and solutions to materials-management challenges. You will need to "work" the systems, analyze strengths and weaknesses, and modify your approach as circumstances and situations change within your classroom environment.

## In this chapter, you will

- discover ways to collect inexpensive and free materials.

- efficiently sort and categorize materials in your classroom.

- determine your storage needs.

- discover innovative storage ideas.

- learn new ways to organize materials for quick and easy access.

- help students learn to find, use, and return materials efficiently.

" Plan your work for today and every day, then work your plan."
—Norman Vincent Peale

# Collecting Materials

**Free and inexpensive materials are readily available if one knows where to look.** Getting donations from parents and local merchants and splitting costs with other teachers not only saves you money, but also emphasizes to students the importance of conserving, recycling, and reusing materials.

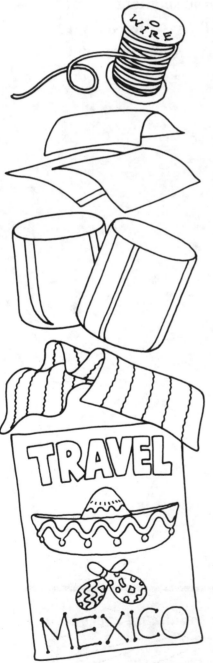

## Money-Saving Tips

- Send a "wish list" to parents and various community organizations as well as relatives and personal friends. Contributions may include games, puzzles, magazines, art supplies, audiotapes, children's books, and large floor pillows. Be specific and emphasize the educational value behind your requests.

- Use Appendix B (pages 128–130) to discover a variety of free or inexpensive materials and "knick-knacks" you can collect. Many retailers are aware of the strained financial conditions of schools and are happy to help. Contact people in the private sector and discuss your needs—be as specific as possible.

- Use Appendix C (pages 131–136) to help you inventory supplies needed for various learning centers. Also, have games readily available for when inclement weather keeps students indoors. Check your school resources for educational games that may be checked out. Have students rotate every month bringing in games to keep in the classroom and share with others. Keep an "Indoor Playtime" card file that includes fun, simple activities (e.g., Heads-Up Seven-Up, 21 Questions, Charades) that you or a substitute may use.

- When making in-person requests for donations, be respectful of the contributor's work schedule. Be prepared to explain the educational purpose behind your request. Let him or her know that donations are tax-deductible and that parents will be told of the generous contributions. Give immediate verbal appreciation for any contribution, then follow up with a written note or letter. Invite students to write thank-you notes to contributors.

- Teachers of the same grade level may find it helpful to buy items in bulk and split the supplies to reduce individual cost. Go to a merchant as a group and be sure to emphasize the educational purpose—this will increase the probability of getting a group rate or discount. Sharing nonconsumable supplies such as scissors, rulers, and calculators with another teacher will also cut costs for classroom materials.

## Recycling Resources

- Use magazine pictures for various art projects or in reading activities to visualize words and concepts.

- Keep a paper recycle bin in your classroom, and have students use discarded paper for scratch paper or art projects.

- Rather than discarding old textbooks, use them for various activities. Have students cut out pictures for different projects; cut apart text to make sequence story cards; or tear out and staple pages into smaller, readable portions.

- Place handwriting-practice papers in plastic protector sheets and reuse. Have students use dry, erasable markers to practice their writing skills.

- Ask parents and community members to donate items such as egg cartons, jars, old silverware, cardboard tubes, fabric scraps, and old clothes for learning centers. Also request old audio- and videotapes that can be taped over and reused.

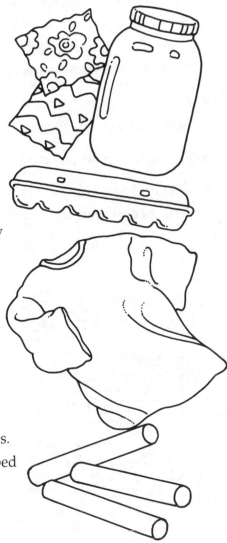

## Super Sub Tub

Every teacher should plan for unexpected absences. Prepare a portable, plastic file box containing three days worth of materials for substitute teachers. Periodically update the materials to keep them current. Include in your sub tub:

- daily and weekly schedules, class lists of students' names, and a seating chart. Include a list of helpful students along with names of "study buddies" (students who work well together).

- administrative forms such as policies and procedures, school employee handbook, and substitute information sheet.

- "teacher's copies" of three read-aloud paperbacks that have been highlighted in helpful ways—important vocabulary words underlined, definitions and pertinent questions written in the margins, and important passages highlighted. Provide materials that stimulate investigation and rereading of the books. Prepare a file folder for each book with suggested activities.

- overhead transparencies with enlarged versions of poems that correlate with the books or current areas of study.

- fun math and art projects that relate to current areas of study.

- a set of the Weekly Reader, student newspapers, or interesting articles copied from a local newspaper for current events.

- a selection of indoor games to play in case of inclement weather.

- an incentive plan for good behavior (e.g., stars, stickers, pencils) so the substitute has tangible rewards available. Also include a note explaining your daily behavior plan so the substitute clearly understands rules and consequences before beginning instruction.

- a special treat for the substitute (e.g., bag of coffee, candy bar) and a small note that simply says, *Thanks for holding down the fort!*

## First-Aid Kit and Emergency Supplies

Every classroom should have a well-supplied first-aid kit, emergency barrels filled with supplies, and emergency procedures posted, including exit instructions. If you are new to the area in which you are teaching, ask questions about procedures for natural disasters (earthquakes, tornadoes, etc.). Research the safety procedures and gather needed supplies. In an emergency, every teacher needs a pair of tennis shoes, a battery-operated radio, and food and water supplies for the classroom. (Check school supplies or emergency items provided by your PTA.) Other miscellaneous items to consider include a sewing kit, plastic garbage bags of all sizes, a loud whistle, "space blankets," and duplicate keys to your car, the classroom, and classroom cabinets.

## Handy Toolbox

Every teacher should have a toolbox in the classroom. By having the right tools handy, you can immediately tend to your classroom needs. Store your toolbox under the classroom sink or in any low cabinet. Do not place heavy tools on top of cabinets where they can fall and cause injury. (You may also choose to lock or secure the toolbox lid to prevent young students from opening it.) Include the following items in your toolbox:

- hammer
- screwdrivers (flat blade and Phillips)
- pliers (regular and needle nose)
- battery-operated drill
- wrenches (crescent and clamp types)

- needle-nose tweezers
- flashlight
- duct tape
- Exacto knife
- wire cutters

## Janitorial Supplies

The same items you have under your sink at home may be helpful at school, such as cleanser, sponges, scouring pads, rags, air freshener, dish-washing tubs, and a drying rack. Store cleaning solution in upper cabinets out of young children's reach. Every classroom also needs a broom and dustpan or a small hand-vac for emergency cleanups.

# Clutter Control

**When sorting and organizing materials, it is helpful to divide the job into smaller, more manageable pieces.** Small tasks accomplished in short periods of time provide a sense of accomplishment and incentive for moving on to the next stage of organization. Before deciding what to keep and what to discard, take inventory of classroom materials and supplies. Categorize items under the following headers:

- Personal Items—coat, umbrella, backpack, coffee mug

- Curriculum Materials—textbooks, workbooks, assessment materials, portfolios

- "Hands-on" Items—games, puzzles, math manipulatives, science kits

- Reference Materials—encyclopedias, dictionaries, trade books

- Equipment—overhead projector, videotapes, tape recorders, record players, headsets, computers, paper cutter, television, VCR

- Small Supplies—paper, pencils, markers, tape, rulers, erasers, hole punch

- PE Supplies—balls, jump ropes, tetherballs

- Art Materials—paints, paintbrushes, newsprint, yarn, construction paper, rubber stamps and stamp pads, craft sticks, fabric scraps

- Odds and Ends—items that do not fit under any other category

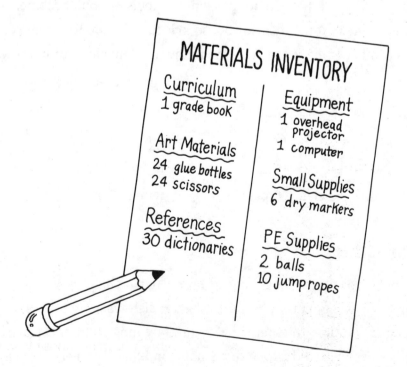

## "Clipboard and Boxes" Sorting System

The Clipboard and Boxes system is ideal for removing years of classroom clutter. Label four boxes *Put It Away, Store It, Repair It,* and *Give It Away.* Use trash bags for the final category, *Throw It Away.* Sort materials in one area of your classroom at a time, placing items in the appropriate box or bag. If you can put away an item while remaining in the same part of the classroom, do so. If putting it away requires you to leave the vicinity, then place the item in the *Put It Away* box and move on to the next item. Place items requiring long-term storage in the *Store-It* box until you are ready to sort and put away items in appropriate storage containers. Work in one-hour increments, sorting items into boxes or bags for 50 minutes, then putting items away for ten. Simplify this procedure by using a rolling cart to move boxes and bags from one area to the next.

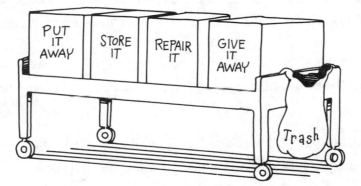

Carry a clipboard for note-taking as you sort and store your supplies—great ideas may come to mind while sorting classroom items. Create a "to-do" list, recording tasks to complete and personal contacts to make after sorting items (e.g., supplies to purchase or collect, storage ideas, who to talk to regarding repairs, comments to make to students about proper care and storage).

As you categorize each classroom object, ask yourself the following questions—an answer of *no* to all questions indicates the item should be discarded.

- *Has anyone used this item in the past year?*

- *Do you attach sentimental value to this item?*

- *Could anyone use this item in the future, especially if you changed grade levels?*

- *Does its value justify the time and energy required to store it?*

- *Do you have space to store the item in your classroom?* (You may choose to explore other storage options on campus.)

## "Active" and "Inactive" Materials

To find stored materials quickly, divide them into two main categories—those used regularly ("active") and those used only periodically ("inactive"). Materials used regularly should be within easy reach. Since "inactive" materials are seldom used, they do not need to be readily accessible. You can store them in sturdy boxes on top of classroom cupboards, in school storage closets, or in other storage areas outside the classroom (e.g., your attic, garage, or storage shed). Be careful about cluttering your personal space at home. If you store something for one or two years and do not use it, give it away or sell it.

## Theme-Related Materials

Store theme-related or seasonal paraphernalia in labeled, sturdy storage boxes. Use one of the following inventory systems to keep track of the items in each container.

- Place an inventory folder in the box that holds the plans for a particular theme. Include a list of the boxed materials, and note the location of theme-related items too large for the box.

- Use the inside of the box lid to record box contents and the location of oversized, theme-related items. Note school and district resources that could be used with this theme.

- Attach library pockets and index cards to the outside of each box to identify the contents. This allows you to check the contents without lifting and moving the boxes.

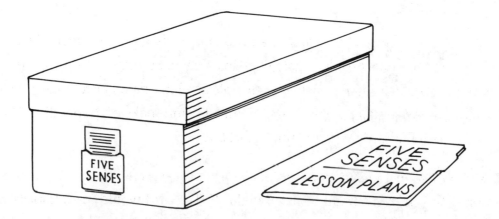

## Assigning Materials to Resource Areas

One of the best ways to organize materials in the classroom is to develop resource areas (classroom library, writing center, science lab, art corner). These areas may consist of cupboards or shelves or individual learning centers. Organize materials by subject matter or thematic units (see Appendix C, pages 131–136). Use colored dots to color-code resource areas with corresponding supplies, making it easier to locate, use, and return items. Also label shelves with words and pictures so the task of finding and putting items back can be delegated to almost anyone. (Picture and word labels also help young students and limited- or non-English speakers practice language skills and expand vocabulary.)

As you organize resource areas, be sure every item is on your materials inventory list. Use 3" x 5" (7.5 cm x 12.5 cm) index cards and a desktop file box to catalog stored materials. List major categories such as *Writing Center* or *Cupboard #4* on divider cards, and list stored items on index cards behind each corresponding category. It's helpful to keep a duplicate inventory card inside each container of supplies for cross-checking. If you don't remember where to find an item, check the card file to see where it's supposed to be.

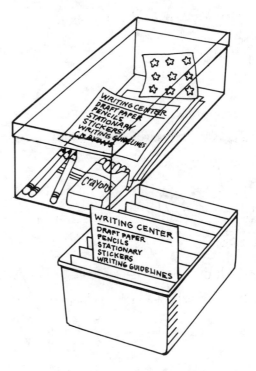

When materials are not used regularly, it is even more difficult to remember their exact location. For that reason, consider cataloging "inactive" materials first—there are usually fewer of these. (You can catalog "active" materials at a later date.) Determine a system for labeling storage boxes, such as *Science #1, #2,* and *#3,* and make corresponding 3" x 5" (7.5 cm x 12.5 cm) file cards with the same labels.

You may choose to include an alphabetical cross-reference section for your card catalogs. For example, *hornets' nests* might be listed under *H.* The card would read, *Hornets' nests— Science Box #3. Hornets' nests* may also be listed under *S* for *Science.* The card would read, *Science Box #3* and list all the contents of the box, including the hornets' nests.

# Storing Materials

**An effective storage system entices students to explore and learn more about specific topics.** Be both practical and creative when storing supplies for student use. Items used together should be stored together. If possible, store materials where they are most often used so you and your students can locate items quickly, reducing classroom "traffic."

- Store learning-center materials by each corresponding station.

- Keep teaching materials close to your desk. If possible, arrange student desks so they are close to their personal cubbies.

- Place art supplies and hands-on science materials close to your classroom sink for easy cleanup.

- Use colorful tubs full of alluring materials specifically labeled to whet students' appetites for learning.

- Store materials on shelves low enough for students to easily find, use, and return.

- Consider using transparent tubs so students can easily see the container's contents before pulling it off the shelf. Also include unusual containers to store supplies, such as a fishing tackle box, large "granny" bag, toolbox, straw basket, or cardboard animal carrier.

- Arrange books related to a new theme face front in the bookshelf with the rest of the classroom library. If you do not have "face-out" book racks, mount brightly-painted rain gutters below chalk trays or door moldings on small "L" brackets. Students will be more apt to reach for books displayed in this fashion.

## Portable Packs

Multipurpose, portable storage containers give you more options and flexibility when arranging and storing supplies. Portable storage also allows students to carry materials anywhere in the room. Portable containers can include:

- Plastic shoe boxes—for individual student supplies, science kits, and loose craft items (yarn, fabric scraps, glitter bottles).

- Coffee cans—to hold small items such as pencils, pens, crayons, markers, and paintbrushes.

- Baskets—can be used to store items that won't fit in other containers.

- Shoe bags—for small, loose items (hole punchers, scissors, calculators), or activities for students to complete independently (math manipulatives, audiotapes, vocabulary card games). They take up little space when attached to a closet door.

- Pocket charts—to hold items such as paperback books, calculators, and a variety of small games (e.g., jacks, cards).

- Lunch boxes—can be repainted or used "as is" to house various thematic materials. For example, a Flintstones lunch box would be a great storage container for a rock collection.

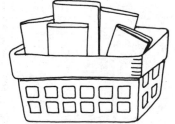

- Plastic gallon or liter bottles—can be used as portable "supply carriers," filled with such items as crayons, pens, scissors, and rulers. Cut out a window in a side panel to provide easy access to the supplies.

- Plastic totes—to hold and transport supplies needed for specific art projects.

## Centralized Supply Stations

When built-in shelves are limited or unavailable, centralized supply stations can house all your art and craft supplies. The illustrated supply station shows organization at its best—neat, labeled, and "user friendly." It is made from a 2' x 4' (60 cm x 120 cm) open cabinet on wheels. Particle-board panels with slotted Masonite™ shelves are used to store construction paper. Stacked boxes (cardboard drawers) placed beside the construction-paper shelves are used to categorize scrap paper into basic colors and their related shades.

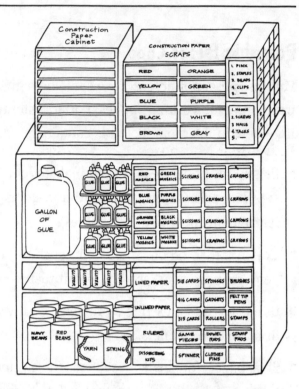

Small plastic drawers organize tiny supplies such as pins, brads, tacks, and so on. Shoe boxes, coffee cans, and plastic-letter trays hold paper, art supplies, and game pieces.

## Rolling Service Carts

Similar to centralized supply stations, rolling carts have a multitude of applications. Use them for storing and transporting technology equipment such as televisions, overhead projectors, tape recorders, and computers. Rolling carts can also be used as mobile art-supply stations. Creative mini-storage containers for your cart may include:

- egg cartons and ice-cube trays for tiny objects.

- kitchen cutlery trays and plastic totes.

- shoe boxes for mini-files.

- plastic tubs for crayons, chalk pieces, etc.

- coffee cans for balls of string, yarn, or ribbon. (Cut a hole in the plastic lid and thread the yarn through. Students can pull out and cut off just what they need while the yarn stays clean inside the can.)

# Paper Sorters, Caddies, and Letter Trays

Paper sorters, caddies, and stackable letter trays provide a multitude of organizational opportunities. They are an essential element of any record-keeping system.

**Individual Mailboxes.** Use a plastic crate filled with hanging folders as "mailboxes" to deliver and receive papers from students. Take-home materials can be stored in each slot. Students can file papers during clean-up time. File parent notices ahead of time so students can pick them up on the way out or retrieve them when they load their backpacks at the end of the day.

**Learning Centers.** Many learning centers benefit from having paper sorters hold individual student work. In a writing center, use slots to house students' writing folders, personalized dictionaries, or specific writing assignments. In a research center, use paper sorters to store ongoing research-report materials—the natural clutter surrounding long-term projects is limited to these slots rather than student desks.

**Supply Towers.** Glue stackable letter trays together to create storage "towers" for games, puzzles, and activities. They can also hold readily-available forms and letters for yourself, your assistant, classroom volunteers, or students (e.g., attendance forms, tardy slips, lunch menus, writing paper, worksheets).

**Communication Caddies.** Attach paper caddies to the classroom door as a quick reminder of what you want to take with you to the administrative office or teachers' lounge. Paper caddies can also store makeup work for absent students—when papers are passed out, the caddie gets one, too. You may also choose to attach a caddie to every desk so students can keep take-home materials separate from their desk materials.

Crate with
Hanging Folders

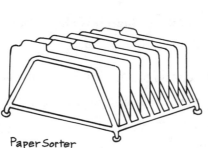

Paper Sorter

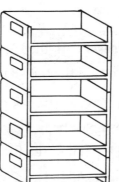

Stackable Trays

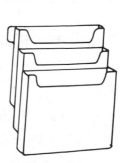

Paper Caddies

## Stack Boxes and Free-Standing Display Boards

Stack boxes are made of cardboard and come flat in two sections—a 10" x 10½" x 3" (25 cm x 26 cm x 7.5 cm) sleeve and a drawer (portable box). Districts often warehouse these storage units so teachers can order them through the district. These cardboard units represent the best in portable storage—math manipulatives, games, center activities, puzzles, etc. can be stored in them, and students can carry them to and from work stations. Glue several sleeves together to make box towers. Paint them with good quality enamel to increase durability and to color-code them with the resource areas in your classroom. Be sure to clearly label all drawers.

Free-standing display boards are ideal for portable learning centers and learning-center activities. They can be used as background displays for student-made museums or science projects. They are also handy surfaces to display completed student assignments such as writing and artwork. The display boards fold out of sight when not in use.

## Big-Book Storage Units

Use special storage units to store big books for beginning readers. Keep them by your class library for easy access.

- Use an old paint easel with the legs cut off as a big-book stand. Store several books on the easel or prop up the books while turning the pages.

- Store big books as well as posters and charts on an abandoned flip-chart rack. Skirt hangers with clips hold the books, posters, or charts, and hangers are held by the closet pole or the top bar of the flip-chart rack.

- Turn a carpenter's sawhorse upside down to create a V-shaped container.

- Hang big books or newspapers over the dowel rods of a portable clothes-drying rack.

# Distributing and Monitoring Materials

**How you distribute and monitor materials can affect the overall operation of your classroom.** The first place to start when devising a distribution system is student desks. Many times, completed work or notes to parents never reach their destination. Instead, they remain hidden in the depths of a student's desk, buried under mounds of books and papers. To counter this "black-hole" phenomenon, consider these suggestions to collect and distribute student materials.

- Conduct a lesson on how to organize desks. Ask students to arrange their textbooks by size, schedule, or subject. Have them store pencils, crayons, markers, paper clips, and other small items in plastic bags or "cigar-type" boxes.

- Choose one day per week in which students clean out their desks, sort papers, take home appropriate papers, and throw away scrap paper.

- For classrooms that use tables instead of desks, store textbooks and related materials in cubbies or baskets on shelves. Have student monitors distribute materials or choose one table at a time to gather their supplies. Use wire baskets to collect all completed work.

- Store subject or unit folders in "work-slot" cabinets—students can retrieve folders from the cabinets as needed.

- Conduct "desk checks" regularly, awarding points or privileges for clean and organized desks. Have an "elf" who, without any warning, checks desks and distributes goodies to those who have clean, well-organized desks.

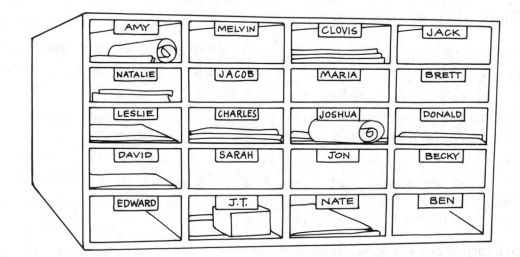

## Student Involvement

Manage materials more efficiently by assigning student jobs. Make job-description cards to define classroom duties (see Appendix D, page 137). You may choose to use pictures instead of words for younger students. For example, a picture of a sink could be the symbol for scouring the sink. Discuss different jobs with students, modeling proper procedures before assigning responsibilities. (See *Assigning Classroom Responsibilities* and *Ways to Assign and Manage Student Jobs*, pages 17–18.) Store job cards in a pocket chart or binder for easy referral.

Record and file a list of jobs each student performs throughout the year. Rotate jobs weekly, bimonthly, monthly, or quarterly to ensure each student completes a variety of tasks. Be sure to allow enough time for students to succeed in their roles before switching responsibilities. You may choose to rotate jobs on different schedules depending on task "popularity." For example, the highly-desired job of distributing PE equipment may be rotated weekly instead of monthly.

Monitor progress as students perform classroom tasks. Record any improvements or additional tasks students accomplish above and beyond the original job descriptions. Encourage time-management practices by having students complete responsibilities within a specific time, gradually decreasing the time allowed as student abilities improve. Compliment students on jobs well done and give pointers to those having difficulty. If some students finish their jobs before the rest of the class, have them help others or "police the grounds" by picking up trash and misplaced items.

# Personal Numbering System

Use the Personal Numbering System to organize and track student materials. Assign numbers based on students' first or last names—the numerical sequence corresponds to ABC order. (If new students join the class, simply add them to the end of the list.) When work is turned in, sequence papers numerically, and "presto"—they are alphabetized for easy entry into your grade book or distribution to student folders.

Explain the Personal Numbering System as you assign numbers to your students. Model and practice using the system, telling students to write their names in the upper left corner of papers and personal numbers on the right. Monitor progress as students use this system. Circulate as students complete work, and look for personal numbers written on every assignment. Use the following pointers to help you manage the Personal Numbering System in your classroom.

- Use the same numbers on report cards, homework, individual student folders, and portfolios to spot missing papers easily. This technique prevents you from having to relabel folders each year—simply reassign numbered materials to new students.

- Numerically label all student cubbies, hanging file folders, individual mailboxes, and take-home envelopes to simplify distribution and collection of materials. Ask students to "mail" their papers by placing them in numbered mailboxes. A glance reveals whether all papers are turned in. Have a student monitor collect the papers, clip them together in numerical order, and place them in the appropriate holding tray for your evaluation.

- Use numbered attendance cards hanging on hooks or placed in library pockets to quickly confirm attendance. Attach student photos on one side of attendance cards and write student numbers on the other. Upon entering the room, have students turn their cards photo forward to verify attendance. Their pictures show all day long until a student monitor turns the cards back to prepare for the next day. Absentees stand out on the attendance board and can be quickly recorded.

- Assign oral-report presentations by number to avoid favoritism. Don't always start with number one. Change the number you start with, but still go in sequence.

- Use personal numbers to assign textbooks and related materials. Store calculators in pocket holders labeled with student numbers.

- Use numbered craft sticks in coffee containers to facilitate lunch count, ask questions to random students, or assign student responsibilities. Simply "pull a number" to select a student for a response or task. Once selected, the craft stick stays out of the can until all sticks have been pulled, giving every student a turn before all sticks are placed back in the can.

- Use Peg-Board with hooks and the Personal Numbering System to store and assign scissors. Use clear mailing tape to secure hooks to the Peg-Board. Write numbers above hooks and on corresponding scissors. (A clear-tape labeler is a good way to mark numbers on scissors.) During clean-up time, each student is responsible for matching his or her scissors to the corresponding hooks—have students place the "ears of the shears" over the hooks.

- Label individual 4-ounce (125-mL) glue bottles, paste canisters (film canisters filled with paste), or glue sticks with student numbers. Store them in tabletop supply baskets, student desks, or a central supply cabinet. Store extra glue (gallon jugs for older students, quart-sized bottles for younger students) at a centralized supply station. Have "glue monitors" refill student glue bottles at clean-up time, as needed.

- Label boxes of markers and crayons with student numbers. Store them in students' desks, tabletop supply baskets, or a central supply station. Place broken crayons or extra markers in cans in your central supply station. If students lose or use up crayons or markers, have them get replacements from the supply station. Any crayons or markers left on the floor are automatically sorted into appropriate cans.

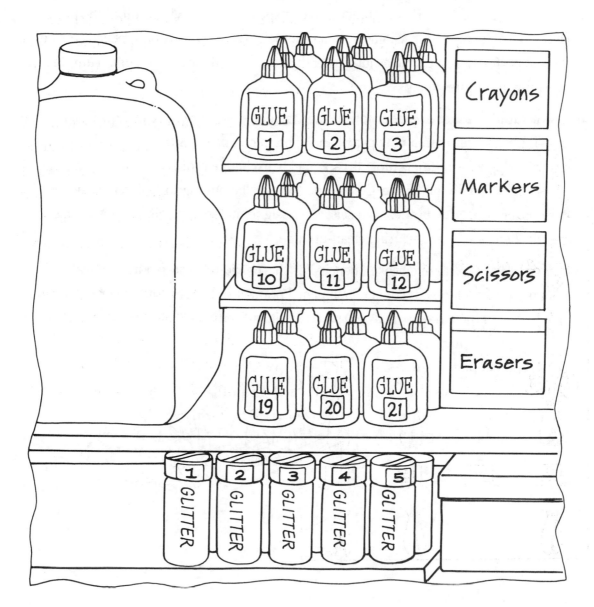

## Resolving Pencil Problems

In every classroom, there is undoubtedly some controversy or chaos pertaining to pencils. Choose from the following options to manage the distribution and use of pencils in your classroom.

- Designate all pencils as community property. Let students enjoy their new pencils for the first few days of school, notifying them that by a certain date, new pencils must be left at home or shared with the class. Invite students to donate their pencils to specific learning centers (e.g., a shark pencil to the Sea Life Center), giving them a sense of pride in their contribution.

- Announce to students that arguments over a specific pencil will result in the pencil being permanently confiscated—it will become part of the classroom pencil collection. This is perfectly acceptable as long as both students and parents are given ample warning about the policy.

- Use a supply basket or plastic tote at each table to distribute pencils. Low baskets that are slightly larger than a new pencil and contain compartmentalized sections work best. During lesson time, students can quickly exchange broken pencils for sharpened ones with virtually no hassle. Color-code supplies belonging to each table, such as pencils, erasers, glue bottles, and scissors. Assign "material monitors" to sharpen pencils before school or during clean-up time.

- Have students exchange broken pencils for sharpened ones stored in a centralized container. Use a low, flat container so pencil points can be seen and retrieved without injury. Never have new pencils in this centralized location—collect short, stubby pencils for this purpose so sharpened pencils are always available but provide no incentive for students to "accidentally" break their pencils.

## Media and Technology Resources

As you face the challenge of bringing technology into an already crowded classroom, it is important to decide how you will use your computer. Having the computer on wheels allows you to move it to any area of the classroom with ease—by your desk for record-keeping, in front of the class for whole-group lessons, or at a learning center for independent practice. Be sure to leave open pathways for moving the computer from one destination to another. Use inexpensive connectors to transmit computer images to a television monitor for easy viewing—this way, you can share captivating software with your whole class rather than two or three students at a time.

Regardless of the type of technology you use (headsets and tape recorders, computers, videotapes), always incorporate a rotation system for using and returning equipment. Consider the following suggestions to help you organize and manage your multi-media centers.

- Use "time cards" to rotate and monitor computer use. Use index cards to make a time card for each student, and store them in a recipe box. Place a timer near the computer and attach a library-book pocket to the side of the monitor to serve as the "time clock." Ask each student to "clock in" before using the computer, writing the starting time on the time card and placing it in the "time-clock" pocket. Have the student set the timer for a specified time period (e.g., ten minutes) and use the computer until time is up. When the timer goes off, have him or her write the ending time on his or her card and place it back in the desktop file before notifying the next student in line.

- Use a yarn "clothesline" and clothespins labeled with personal numbers to track and monitor use of computers, audio headsets, and other equipment. When the timer indicates time is up, the student simply unclips his or her clothespin and puts it in a can.

- Give each student a blank computer disk to store computer-generated assignments. Store disks in a container next to the computer for easy access.

# Materials Management Review

## Did you:

 gather essential materials by enlisting the help of colleagues, parents, and local merchants?

 use the "Clipboard and Boxes" system for clutter control?

 categorize materials as "active" or "inactive," assigning them to corresponding resource areas and recording stored items on inventory cards?

☑ use multipurpose, portable storage containers to store materials?

 implement a variety of systems to simplify the transportation and storage of materials?

☑ efficiently distribute and monitor materials, supplies, and equipment without wasting time or interrupting instruction?

☑ train students to manage materials by defining, assigning, clarifying, and reinforcing expectations?

☑ develop a rotation system to manage student use of media and technology resources?

*" Nothing is particularly hard*
*if you divide it into smaller jobs."*
—Henry Ford

# PAPERWORK MANAGEMENT

Teachers consistently rate paperwork as their number-one management problem. It is part of almost every aspect of teaching—planning, instruction, student motivation, communication, and evaluation.

You cannot escape paperwork in the teaching profession. However, you can learn to handle the plethora of paperwork more efficiently and discover alternative assessment methods that reduce the number of papers crossing your desk.

## In this chapter, you will

- learn to reduce paperwork and still provide effective feedback.

- gain tips for organizing files.

- discover file systems that help in planning and implementing.

- learn how to sort teacher mail quickly and efficiently.

> **" What the world really needs is more love and less paperwork. "**
> **—Pearl Bailey**

# Reducing Paperwork

**Although correcting and sorting paperwork is unavoidable, there are several teaching strategies and techniques you can use to limit the number of papers that cross your desk.** The following ideas are just a few simple ways to reduce and manage paperwork in your classroom.

## Alternative Teaching Techniques

**Decrease the Number of Grades Given.** It is not necessary to collect and check all practice papers. Much insight and learning is accomplished by simply monitoring students as they complete independent work, offering immediate, on-the-spot assistance as needed. Students benefit more from one-to-one interactions than from the amount of time you spend looking through massive amounts of corrected papers. A practical rule of thumb is to take only one grade per week per content area for each student. This step alone will cut the number of papers you grade.

**Limit the Number of Problems Assigned.** When a collection of written work is needed for portfolios or corrected-work packets, have students complete just a few problems off the chalkboard rather than extensive amounts of practice problems. Three or four problems are more than enough to assess understanding.

**Teach and Test Critical Attributes.** Determine the critical attributes of each new concept before instruction, then focus on these key points when teaching lessons. For example, when teaching about mammal characteristics, a long list could be generated; however, two attributes are the most critical—hair and mammary glands. By having your students focus on critical attributes, then testing for understanding on only these key points, you will reduce your workload while still providing essential information.

**Teach Integrated Lessons.** Rather than teaching each subject as an isolated unit, consider teaching integrated units and assessing written assignments for multiple skills. For example, have students write a story about mammals as part of a science unit, then check their work for understanding of science concepts as well as general writing structure, spelling, and grammar.

**Use Quick-Check Papers and Materials.** If you want written documentation, have students write plus or minus signs to indicate answers to "yes/no" questions spoken aloud or written on an overhead. Use ten or twenty items so scores can be quickly calculated by you or your students as a percentage. Purchase "quick-check" materials that allow students to self-pace and monitor their progress, such as multiplication flash cards or computer software that scores overall response.

**Streamline Tests and Assignments.** Make a place for answers on the right-hand side of papers. Have students work through problems, then write answers in the "answers only" section. This allows you to quickly check correct responses.

| MATH PROBLEMS | | Answers |
|---|---|---|
| 1. 14 ×8 | 2. 12 ×2 | 1. _____ |
| | | 2. _____ |
| 3. 17 ×9 | 4. 11 ×8 | 3. _____ |
| | | 4. _____ |
| 5. 22 ×4 | 6. 14 ×11 | 5. _____ |
| | | 6. _____ |
| 7. 12 ×5 | 8. 16 ×6 | 7. _____ |
| | | 8. _____ |

**Use Oral Practice.** Have students share their understanding through oral discussion and hand signals. For example, have students use "thumbs up" or "thumbs down" to indicate agreement or disagreement with given information. Invite students to answer multiple-choice questions by holding up one, two, or three fingers to indicate agreement with the first, second, or third choice. (To ensure individual accountability, have students close their eyes before giving responses.) Use a class roster to check off understanding, placing a minus sign by students who responded incorrectly, highlighting those needing extra help. Be sure to announce correct answers immediately after responses are given.

What is 5 × 12 ?
- (A) 48
- (B) 60
- (C) 50

**Train Volunteers.** Train adult volunteers to help students with both written and oral practice. Emphasize the importance of guiding and encouraging students to think through their responses before giving answers. Have helpers use answer keys to circle incorrect responses, writing correct answers beside each incorrect problem before returning papers for final review.

## Student-Corrected Work

Even younger students can learn to correct their own papers, first through whole-class guided instruction and later individually at a "grading station." Have students place pencils in their desks and use a colored crayon, pencil, or pen to check their responses—either by listening to answers given aloud or with an answer key. Ask students to circle incorrect responses, write correct answers nearby, then rework the problems. To ensure students follow along, have them place dots next to correct answers. Walk around and monitor students as they check their work, emphasizing the importance of honesty when self-checking papers and the knowledge gained from errors. Invite students scoring 100% to offer their papers as extra answer keys or help monitor others' progress. After self-checking is complete, scan corrected papers for accuracy and overall understanding.

## Partner-Checking Techniques

- Invite students to read aloud to partners. Students enjoy this activity and easily correct each others' errors and overall understanding as they retell the story in their own words. Before having students read to partners, model behavior and clarify specific expectations. As students read, monitor their progress and offer encouragement.

- Have student pairs tape-record their reading sessions. Students will benefit from hearing themselves read (i.e., listening for oral expression and reading fluency), and you will have taped sessions to use for individual assessment.

- Have students peer-edit initial writing stages. Divide the class into small teams. First, have authors check their own papers for errors, one concept at a time (e.g., spelling, punctuation, content), then at a signal, have them pass papers to students on their left who then recheck the work. Repeat the process until each paper has been checked by three or four different people. Encourage students to use resources to help edit papers (e.g., dictionaries, encyclopedias, personal spelling booklets). After peer-editing is complete, have authors rewrite the papers and give them to you. Recognize and reward those groups that do thorough and accurate peer-editing.

- Have partners write in journals step-by-step procedures they use to solve one or two problems written on the chalkboard. Discuss answers orally and collect journals to check written work.

- Rather than assigning math story problems for students to complete, have them generate their own (with answers on the back) for partners to solve.

- Invite students to complete math problems with partners. While half the students figure the problem on paper, have partners calculate answers using calculators. Ask pairs to compare results before switching roles—if partners agree, they continue with the next problem; if not, they switch roles and repeat the process. If partners still don't agree, have them save the problem until all other problems are complete, then turn to you or student monitors for help. Ask partners to do a final check at a grading table, circling any errors and returning to their seats to rework incorrect answers.

- Have partners split assignments in half—one person completing the odd-numbered problems, the other completing the even. As one partner works on a problem, the other watches and offers support. Have students verbalize what they are doing as they complete each problem, sharing insights with partners as well as with you as you walk around and monitor progress.

# Recording Student Progress

**The most important reason for keeping records is quick access to student information and on-target planning for future learning experiences.** Consider your current record-keeping systems and ask yourself the following questions:

- *Do my records communicate what students have learned?*

- *Can I use my current records for planning future learning experiences?*

- *Are my current record-keeping systems efficient and easy to use?*

## "One-Stop" Record System

The ease of record keeping is lost when teachers flip through grade books, trying to locate where different grades have been recorded. Save time (and frustration) by using the "one-stop" record system—allocating several lines in your grade book to each student, then recording several marks together in one spot. This approach is appropriate for older students if you are teaching one subject in a departmentalized system.

To set up the "one-stop" system, write the date and days of the week on the horizontal axis of the record sheet as you would for traditional record keeping (see Record Sheet reproducible, page 125.) List student names vertically on the left side of the page, skipping about six lines between each entry—you will fit about five student names per page. Record performance marks on each line as follows:

| Quarter: 1ST   Subject: MATH | | 10/7 | 8 | 9 | 10 | 11 | 10/14 | 15 | 16 | 17 | 18 | 10/19 | 20 |
|---|---|---|---|---|---|---|---|---|---|---|---|---|---|
| Date | | | | | | | | Test 7 | Quiz 3 | | | | |
| **Name** | | Test 4 | | | | | | | | | | | |
| | | | A | A | | T | | T | A | | | | |
| Backer, Cassie | ATTEND/TARDY | | | 2 | | | | 3 | | | | | |
| 12345 Anystreet | RULES | I | | | − | + | + | + | + | − | | | |
| Anytown, CA 67891 | PARTICIPATION | | + | | | | | | | | | | |
| PHONE# 555-5252 | HOMEWORK | 10 | 10 | 10 | 10 | 9 | 10 | 10 | 8 | 10 | 10 | | |
| TESTS, QUIZES, WORKSHEETS | | | 95/100 | | | 90/100 | | 60/60 | | | | | |
| ACCUMULATIVE POINTS EARNED | | 10 | 115 | 125 | 135 | 234 | 244 | 314 | | | | | |
| ACCUMULATIVE POINTS AVAILABLE | | 10 | 120 | 130 | 140 | 250 | 260 | 330 | | | | | |

- Record attendance and tardies on the first line—*A* for absent, *T* for tardy, or blank if students arrive to class on time.

- Use the second line to track rules broken that day. For example, if a student fails to abide by your #2 rule, write a numeral 2 in the grade book for that day. Blank spaces indicate students are following the rules.

- The third line is for recording participation—use plus and minus signs for above-average and below-average involvement; indicate average participation with blank boxes or check marks.

- Record credit for homework on the fourth line. Use point values rather than letter grades (an "85" rather than a "B" grade) to tally and determine final scores.

- Use the fifth line to record scores for that day's in-class assignment, quiz, or test. Again, numbers are much easier to tally and total.

- Use the sixth line to record the accumulative running total of points earned, so at a moment's notice, you may check the current grade for each student. Encourage older students to keep their own running tally and then compare it to the scores recorded in your grade book.

## Multi-Folder Record System

The multi-folder record system is an effective way to monitor student progress, especially when tracking step-by-step concepts and skills. To best use this system, it is important to know your curriculum and plan in advance. Identify the concepts and skills you plan to teach for each subject, then identify which lessons to teach within each time frame (daily, weekly, or monthly). Make a separate folder for each content area, or place several content areas in one folder. Prepare legal-sized record folders for each quarter, or use the same folders to record marks for the entire year.

Use a simple class grid (Record Sheet reproducible, page 125) to list students' names down the left side and concepts or skills to be learned across the top. Use an X on the record sheet to indicate mastery of a skill or concept, and a diagonal line (half of an X) to identify work in progress. After introducing a new concept and providing guided practice, give each student a diagonal mark on the record sheet. When a student masters the skill, change the diagonal to an X.

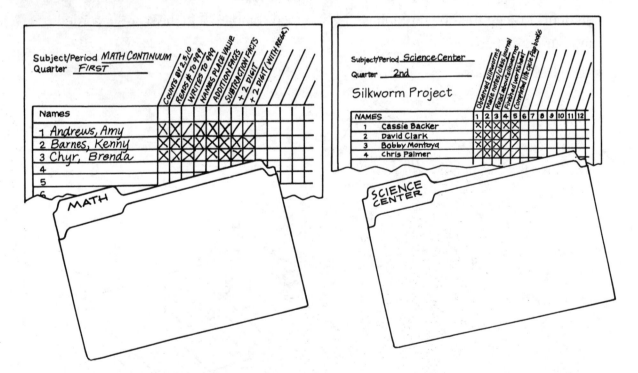

Examine your report card to determine the core of your record-keeping system. Student needs will determine other areas of evaluation to include in your system. If your report cards do not match the way student progress is recorded on a daily basis, you may wish to give parents an additional assessment grid that shows progress on specific skills.

# Setting Up Files

**The files you keep within easy reach should contain important information pertaining to administrative protocols, student information, and curriculum planning.** Your goal is to find any information you have in a file folder within three minutes—less for computer files. Use the following suggestions to help you set up and organize files quickly and easily.

## Fast Filing Tips

- Start new files with broad subjects such as *Math* or *Language Arts*, then divide into subcategories such as *Number Facts, Geometry*, and *Measurement* (see Appendix E, page 138, for generic titles).

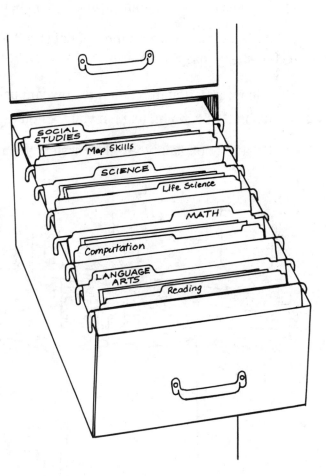

- For quick file retrieval, use all capital letters for major category labels and lowercase titles for subdivisions.

- Use labeled hanging folders arranged in alphabetical order for major subject areas. Use manila folders to group subcategories and organize them within hanging folders by topic alphabetically or by the order they are scheduled in your day.

- Folders should be about two inches thick before you subdivide—keep in mind that many thin folders with precise titles may be difficult to remember and locate among the numerous files you accumulate.

- If you have access to a computer, make labels the size and font of your choice on sheets of self-sticking labels.

- If you decide to color-coordinate your files, hand-print all subheading labels in each category with the same-colored felt-tip pen (e.g., *Story Sequence* and *Vocabulary* written in red) for easy file retrieval and replacement.

- Group materials used for the same lesson in a single file. For example, if you always use a particular trade book to teach poetry, place it with the corresponding lesson plans in the same file. If you have a section of your files dedicated to specific skill lessons, make a note in the file folder about the location of corresponding materials.

- Tape an index card on the front of each file drawer or storage unit listing the enclosed files.

- File information in relation to how you use it—the more often you use it, the closer it should be to you (e.g., in your bottom desk drawer).

- Be sure to explain your filing system to parent volunteers and student helpers.

## "Can't-Miss" Classroom Files

**Curriculum-Planning Files.** Set up files to hold your "working" curriculum—your personal collection of lessons. Provide a separate section for each content area. Include in each file a list of critical concepts and skills to teach throughout the year as well as copies of your current lesson plans and comments about each lesson's strengths and weaknesses. (Record comments after teaching each lesson, while experiences are still clear in your mind. This will reduce the amount of planning needed for the upcoming year.) Also include copies of unit plans and inventories that correlate to stored materials (e.g., where supportive materials for a lesson are stored in the classroom). These "reminders" save you the time and aggravation of rummaging through supplies.

**Individual Student Files.** In a separate portable "folder holder," away from student access, maintain an individual file folder for each student. These student files should not be confused with portfolios, which are collections of student work. Individual student folders contain confidential records of ongoing communication with parents and/or support staff regarding a particular student. Use this file system to store pertinent information about each child in your classroom.

**"Administrivia" Files.** Place administrative papers such as PTA newsletters, agendas for upcoming faculty meetings, and the principal's daily bulletin into their own folders for easy retrieval. Also use this file to store documents such as parent permission slips, requisition forms, and conference reminders.

**Electronic Files.** Electronic files are valuable for storing important items such as student records, correspondence logs, lesson plans, and computer-generated curriculum. When organizing electronic files, be sure to follow the same principle used with paper files—working from the broadest categories to the smallest. For example, include "folders" such as *Parents*, *Students*, and *Administration* within an electronic file folder called *CORRESPONDENCE*. Remember to delete old, out-of-date information.

**"Tickler" Files.** "Tickler" files contain materials you discover in the course of teaching that you anticipate using in the future. Monthly tickler files are a valuable planning device as well as an excellent way to organize your loose curriculum papers. Write the names of the months on ten or twelve different file folders (depending on your teaching year). As you find information you anticipate using during a particular month (e.g., seasonal poetry, activities, fun facts), slip it into that month's "tickler" folder. Store monthly tickler folders in portable "folder holders," rotating the folders after each month (keeping the most current month in front).

Store weekly folders (labeled by week number) in front of the monthly tickler folders. At the beginning of each month, sort the collected materials into weekly folders, anticipating which materials you plan to use each week. Place the weekly folders for the current month in a separate, vertical wire rack for easier access. Use these folders to plan your daily lessons, pulling needed materials from the folders before beginning instruction each day. (You may also choose to keep a "day" folder at your desk to store materials being used that day. At the end of the day, place materials no longer needed back into the month's tickler file.)

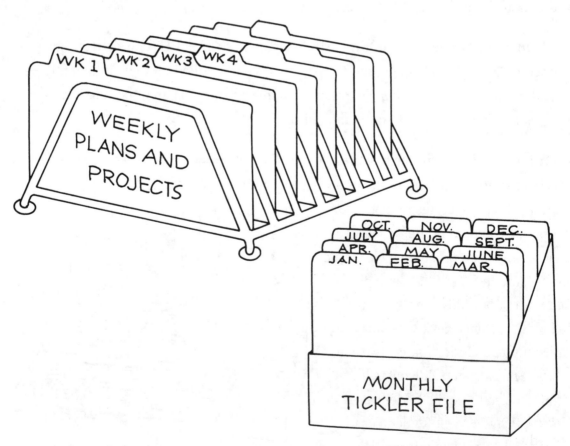

# Organizing Teacher Mail

**A five-tiered, horizontal desktop file and a "round file" (i.e., trash can) are all you need to categorize your miscellaneous papers.** Label the top tier of the desktop file *IN*, the second *HOLD*, the third *DO*, the fourth *FILE*, and the bottom *READ*. Throw away any papers you don't need and place all remaining mail in the *IN* slot until you have a moment to sort through it. Don't wait too long—set aside time each day to complete this task.

- **IN**—This slot holds your mail until you are ready to sort and file.

- **HOLD**—Use this slot for materials or notices being referred to someone else (i.e., a colleague, administrator, parent, or student). When holding materials for others, place a stick-on note with the recipient's name on the corresponding material as a reminder.

- **DO**—In this slot, store any notices that require a decision or action such as calling about a book order, responding to a workshop brochure, recording important dates onto your calendar, or returning parent phone calls.

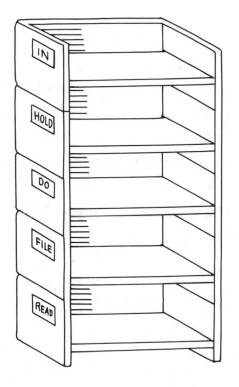

- **FILE**—Use this slot to store materials to be filed for future use, such as catalogs, administrative protocols, school directories, and PTA agendas.

- **READ**—Place in this slot articles and resource materials that require longer than a few minutes to read.

After sorting items into their slots, take action. First, concentrate on the *DO* section—reading bulletins, writing appointments on your calendar, filling out requisition forms, and responding to phone calls. Next, check your *HOLD* file and distribute collected materials. Save yourself time by dropping materials for colleagues in their mailboxes as you leave for home, or distributing items at staff meetings. Finally, file papers from the *FILE* tray into the appropriate folders. Ideally, you should file papers at least once a week. When possible, delegate tasks to others. Place stick-on notes on materials to explain procedures to helpers.

# Paperwork Management Review

## Did you:

☑ reduce your paperwork by using alternative methods for checking and assessing student progress?

☑ use the "one-stop" and/or multi-folder record-keeping system to organize, retrieve, and add to recorded grades?

☑ use a clear and distinctive labeling system to organize files?

☑ set up files using broad categories before dividing into subdivisions?

☑ set up file systems to group and organize similar files (administrative files, student files, curriculum-planning files, electronic files)?

☑ sort, categorize, and file teacher mail promptly?

*" Persistence and determination alone are omnipotent. The slogan "press on" has solved, and will always solve, the problems of the human race."*

—*Calvin Coolidge*

# Daily Planner

_____
(date)

✔ = complete          ● = in progress          ➜ = forward to tomorrow

Things to do **before** school:

☐ _____

☐ _____

☐ _____

Things to do **at school** in the morning:

☐ _____

☐ _____

☐ _____

☐ _____

Things to do **at school** in the afternoon:

☐ _____

☐ _____

☐ _____

☐ _____

Things to do **after** school:

☐ _____

☐ _____

☐ _____

# Welcome Back!

Dear _____,

Inside this folder is the work you missed.
When you have a chance to catch up, please
give your completed work to me inside this
folder. The worksheets and paper you will need
are enclosed. Please complete this work by

_____.

**Reading**                                    Check box
                                               when complete

_____

_____        ☐


**Language/Spelling**

_____

_____        ☐


**Math**

_____

_____        ☐


**Science/Social Studies**

_____

_____        ☐


**Other**

_____

_____        ☐


I have finished all my makeup work.

Signed _____ Date _____

# Let's Get Acquainted!

Child's Name _____ Birthdate _____

Parents' Names _____

Address _____

_____

Home Phone _____ Work Phone _____

Names of other family members (including pets):

_____

_____

_____

List several of your child's "favorites," such as a favorite food, TV show, book, or hobby:

_____

_____

Your child's strengths:

_____

_____

Areas needing improvement:

_____

_____

Educational needs of your child from your perspective:

_____

_____

Any other information you would like to provide:

_____

_____

# Name Search

**Welcome to Room** _____!

Name _____ Date _____

**Directions:** Write classmates' names vertically, horizontally, or diagonally, with one letter per box. You may work alone, with a partner, or in teams. Give the filled-out sheet to a friend and invite him or her to look for and circle the names.

# Helping Hands

# Helping Hands

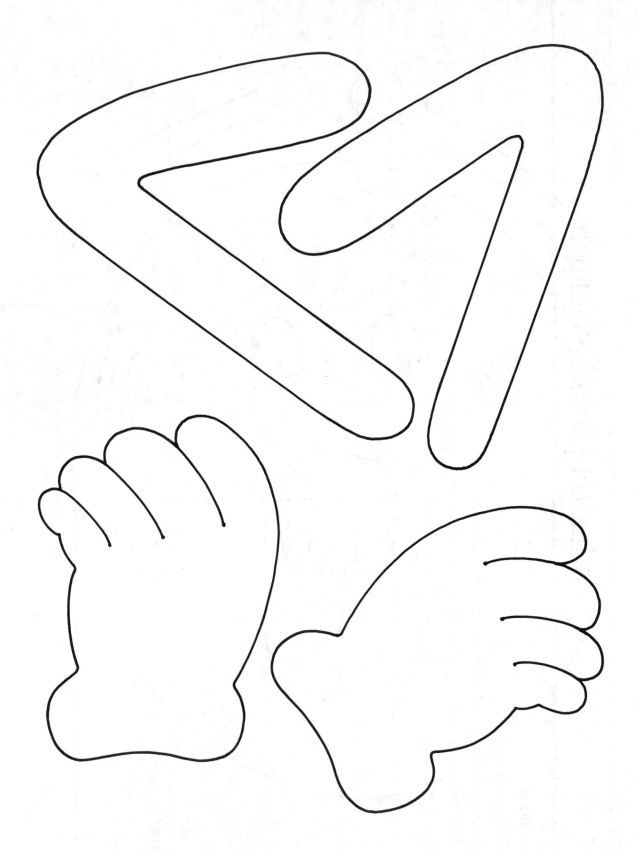

People Management

Name _____  Date _____

# Estimating Accomplishments

**Directions:**

1. Write your goal.
2. Estimate how long it will take to complete the goal.
3. Write how much time it actually took to complete the goal.
4. Record your thoughts about reaching your goal and discuss them with a classmate.

## Estimating Chart

| Goal | Estimated Time | Actual Time | Comments |
|------|----------------|-------------|----------|
| Goal |                |             |          |
| Goal |                |             |          |
| Goal |                |             |          |
| Goal |                |             |          |

# Personal Learning Log

| Goal | Date Started | Expected Finish Date | Actual Finish Date | Comments |
|------|--------------|----------------------|--------------------|----------|
|      |              |                      |                    |          |
|      |              |                      |                    |          |
|      |              |                      |                    |          |
|      |              |                      |                    |          |
|      |              |                      |                    |          |
|      |              |                      |                    |          |
|      |              |                      |                    |          |
|      |              |                      |                    |          |
|      |              |                      |                    |          |
|      |              |                      |                    |          |
|      |              |                      |                    |          |
|      |              |                      |                    |          |
|      |              |                      |                    |          |
|      |              |                      |                    |          |

Name _____

# Daily Work Goals

|  | Reading | Language Arts | Math | Science/ Social Studies | Other | Comments |
|---|---|---|---|---|---|---|
| Monday |  |  |  |  |  |  |
| Tuesday |  |  |  |  |  |  |
| Wednesday |  |  |  |  |  |  |
| Thursday |  |  |  |  |  |  |
| Friday |  |  |  |  |  |  |

# Choosing Time Journal

Name _____

Date _____

My choice is _____
_____
_____

I chose this because _____
_____
_____

The way I feel about my choice now is _____
_____
_____

✂ - - - - - - - - - - - - - - - - - - - - - - - - - - - - - - - - - - - - - - - - - -

# Choosing Time Journal

Name _____

Date _____

My choice is _____
_____
_____

I chose this because _____
_____
_____

The way I feel about my choice now is _____
_____
_____

Name _____

# Backward Planning

Month _____

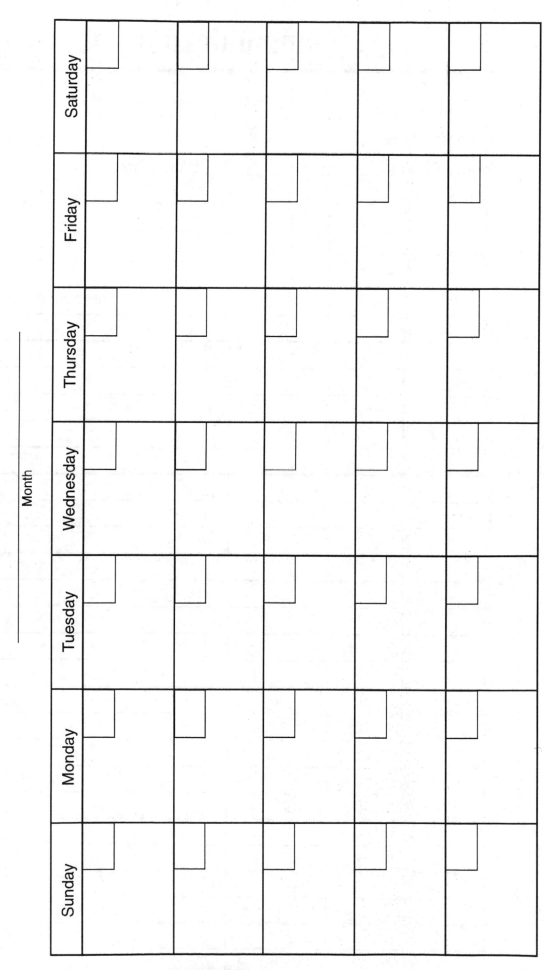

| Sunday | Monday | Tuesday | Wednesday | Thursday | Friday | Saturday |
|--------|--------|---------|-----------|----------|--------|----------|
|        |        |         |           |          |        |          |
|        |        |         |           |          |        |          |
|        |        |         |           |          |        |          |
|        |        |         |           |          |        |          |
|        |        |         |           |          |        |          |

# Communication Log

Student's Name _____

Parents' Names _____

Home Phone _____ Work Phone _____

Family Data _____

_____

Health Issues _____

| Date | Subject | Response |
|------|---------|----------|
|      |         |          |
|      |         |          |
|      |         |          |
|      |         |          |
|      |         |          |
|      |         |          |
|      |         |          |
|      |         |          |
|      |         |          |
|      |         |          |
|      |         |          |
|      |         |          |
|      |         |          |
|      |         |          |
|      |         |          |
|      |         |          |
|      |         |          |
|      |         |          |
|      |         |          |
|      |         |          |
|      |         |          |
|      |         |          |
|      |         |          |
|      |         |          |
|      |         |          |
|      |         |          |

# Homework Assignment Sheet

Name _____    Week of _____

| Day of the Week | Assignment | Parent's Initials |
|---|---|---|
| Monday | | |
| Tuesday | | |
| Wednesday | | |
| Thursday | | |
| Friday | | |

Comments:

_____

_____

_____

# Self-Evaluation Log

Work Sample: _____ Date: _____

What I Did: _____

_____

_____

Why I Chose this Sample: _____

_____

_____

What I Learned: _____

_____

_____

What I Would Do Differently: _____

_____

_____

✂ - - - - - - - - - - - - - - - - - - - - - - - - - - - - - - - - - - - - - - - - - - - - - - - - - - - - - - - -

Work Sample: _____ Date: _____

What I Did: _____

_____

_____

Why I Chose this Sample: _____

_____

_____

What I Learned: _____

_____

_____

What I Would Do Differently: _____

_____

_____

# Record Sheet

**Subject/Period** _____

| Student Name | Date | | | | | | | | | | | | | | |
|---|---|---|---|---|---|---|---|---|---|---|---|---|---|---|---|
| | | | | | | | | | | | | | | | |
| | | | | | | | | | | | | | | | |
| | | | | | | | | | | | | | | | |
| | | | | | | | | | | | | | | | |
| | | | | | | | | | | | | | | | |
| | | | | | | | | | | | | | | | |
| | | | | | | | | | | | | | | | |
| | | | | | | | | | | | | | | | |
| | | | | | | | | | | | | | | | |
| | | | | | | | | | | | | | | | |
| | | | | | | | | | | | | | | | |
| | | | | | | | | | | | | | | | |
| | | | | | | | | | | | | | | | |
| | | | | | | | | | | | | | | | |
| | | | | | | | | | | | | | | | |
| | | | | | | | | | | | | | | | |
| | | | | | | | | | | | | | | | |
| | | | | | | | | | | | | | | | |
| | | | | | | | | | | | | | | | |
| | | | | | | | | | | | | | | | |
| | | | | | | | | | | | | | | | |
| | | | | | | | | | | | | | | | |
| | | | | | | | | | | | | | | | |
| | | | | | | | | | | | | | | | |
| | | | | | | | | | | | | | | | |
| | | | | | | | | | | | | | | | |

# Appendix A—Classroom Leadership Jobs

**Audio-Visual Helper**—sets up and puts away tape recorders, filmstrip projector, overhead projector, TV monitor, and videotapes.

**Center Group Leader**—facilitates problem-solving at learning centers.

**Class Secretary**—records agreements or solutions formulated by the class.

**Courier**—carries messages from the classroom to the office or other classrooms.

**First Aid Captain**—in charge of minor situations in which bandages or other basic first-aid supplies might be needed.

**Guest Greeter**—answers the door and introduces guests to the class.

**Homework Helper**—takes care of paperwork for daily homework.

**Horticulturist**—learns about and takes care of classroom plants.

**Keeper of the Journals**—responsible for distributing and collecting journals.

**Leadership Chart Keeper**—rotates "special job" cards as directed by the teacher.

**Lights Helper**—turns classroom lights on and off when needed.

**Line Leader**—leads the class to and from recess, lunch, special assemblies, and so on.

**Lunch Monitor**—takes lunch orders and milk count. Takes money to the cafeteria.

**Marine Biologist**—learns about and takes care of classroom fish.

**People Management**

**Math Checker**—checks other students' drill activities. (May have to work during recess.)

**Party Planner**—helps plan holiday celebrations and sets guidelines for parties.

**PE Equipment Monitor**—distributes play equipment during recess and PE.

**President**—presides over class meetings and daily opening exercises.

**Student Editor**—edits other students' work.

**Subject Secretary**—takes care of paperwork for specific subjects.

**"Sunshine" Keeper**—writes notes or cards to class members who are ill, or places hand-made cards from students into a large envelope in preparation for delivery.

**Table Leader**—facilitates any table task.

**Teacher's Middle Desk Drawer Monitor**—cleans and restocks supplies in the drawer.

**Telephone Monitor**—answers the telephone and takes or relays messages.

**Treasurer**—keeps track of class funds, collects fund-raiser materials, and sometimes takes lunch count and money.

**Vice President**—presides in the absence of the president and leads the flag salute.

**Welcome Team**—committee that welcomes and supports new students.

**Window Operator**—opens and closes windows when needed.

**Zoologist**—learns about and takes care of classroom animals.

# Appendix B—Free and Inexpensive Materials

Airlines—"wings" (rewards), magazines, courtesy kits

Bank—coin wrappers, maps, pencils

Business—computers, computer software, storage bins, boxes, cabinets

Carpet store—carpet scraps, cardboard, cardboard tubes

Caterer—leftover crepe paper, party supplies

Contractor—scrap lumber, boards, plastic pipes, bricks

Dentist—toothbrushes, posters, pamphlets, old magazines

Department store—post-holiday decorations, damaged merchandise

Drugstore—lightweight units, card stands, magazine racks

Dry cleaner—hangers, plastic bags

Electrician—electrical wire, small pieces of conduit, electrical spools

Fabric shop—heavy cardboard tubes, cloth scraps

Farmer—burlap bags, grains, biological specimens, twine

Florist—floral wrapping paper, ribbon, plants

Fruit stand—orange crates, plastic fruit baskets, cardboard vegetable baskets

Garage sale—books, magazines, toys, storage bins, dishpans, old appliances, bookcases, bureaus, cabinets, trunks, serving carts

**Hairdresser**—wigs, cosmetics

**Hardware store**—used mixing buckets,
tote boxes, toolboxes

**Hospital**—pill bottles, various containers,
tongue depressors, health literature

**Liquor store**—cardboard boxes with dividers,
cartons, boxes

**Lumber yard**—Peg-Board, dowels, clay flue pipes,
scrap boards, nail aprons, yardsticks, rulers, metal bands

**Motel/Hotel**—linen, soap, matches, cups, notepads, pencils

**Moving and storage company**—wardrobe boxes, cartons

**Newspaper office**—newsprint from roll ends,
photos, film canisters

**Nursing home**—pill bottles, boxes

**Paint store**—wallpaper samples, paint,
paint-mixing sticks, yardsticks, buckets

**Parents/Home**—covered containers (coffee cans,
toolboxes, plastic containers), egg cartons, shoe boxes,
milk cartons, onion bags, old or used furniture, carpeting,
books, fabric, clothing, old shirts for smocks, wallpaper
scraps, yarn, used audio- and videotapes, cooking
utensils, used stamps, pill bottles, cardboard shirt boxes,
old magazines, catalogs

**Photography store**—film canisters, outdated film

**Pizza parlor**—pizza boxes, round cardboard plates

**Plasterer**—5-gallon (25L) buckets

**Plumber**—plastic pipe scrap

**Post office**—stamp posters, outdated FBI wanted posters

**Printer**—paper, card stock, ink, cardboard boxes with lids

**Professor**—books, journals, used computer disks, computer printout paper

**Radio/TV repair shop**—magnets, wires, electrical parts, knobs

**Radio/TV station**—records, CDs, discarded film, used audio- and videotapes, slides

**Real estate company**—notepads, calendars, local maps

**Restaurant**—plastic containers with lids, corks, party supplies, straws, paper cups, coupons, posters, napkins, bottles, ice-cream vats, paper menus, cardboard take-out containers

**Supermarket**—milk crates, pie or cake racks, egg crates, berry baskets, shelving, paper bags, plastic bags, Styrofoam trays, cardboard display units

**Tailor**—cloth scraps, empty thread spools

**Theatre**—tickets, movie posters, promotion photos

**Travel agent**—travel posters, maps, out-of-date travel books

**Upholsterer**—fabric scraps, thread

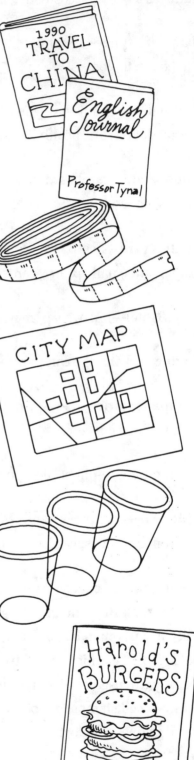

# Appendix C—Recommended Materials for Learning Centers

## Reading Corner

- area rug
- beanbags
- books (variety of topics and sizes)
- book baskets (to categorize books)
- bookshelves
- date stamps and pads
- flannel board and props
- games and puzzles
- globes or maps
- index-card catalog (to check out books)
- magazines
- pencils (regular and colored)
- pillows
- pocket charts
- poetry charts
- reading logs
- reference books
- response journals
- rocking chair
- work cubbies

## Research Center (The "Finding Out" Center)

- completed work samples (graphs, research reports, inquiry letters)
- holding trays (for storing work)
- index-card file on theme-related questions
- paper (notepads, graph paper, stationery)
- pencils (regular and colored)
- phone books
- reference books
- science equipment
- tables and chairs
- tape recorders and headsets

## Writing Center

- adding-machine tape
- bookshelves
- clipboards
- crayons and markers
- date stamps and pads
- electric pencil sharpener
- envelopes
- erasers
- greeting cards
- index cards
- individual work cubbies
- laptop chalkboards
- letter stamps
- magazines
- paper trays
- paper (all types, sizes, and shapes)
- pencils (regular and colored)
- pens (regular and calligraphy)
- plastic magnetic letters
- pocket chart with skill cards
- publishing materials and supplies
- rebus story cards
- reference books (dictionaries, thesauruses, etc.)
- reference charts
- scissors
- table and chairs
- typewriter or computer
- writing folders

## Design and Discover Center

- computer software
- construction crafts (building blocks and logs, toothpicks and gumdrops, cardboard, etc.)
- crayons and markers
- drafting tools
- erector sets
- paper
- paper trays
- pencils (regular and colored)
- reference books (designing techniques, architecture, famous discoveries, etc.)
- rolling file crate with hanging folders (for record keeping)
- rulers
- tables and chairs

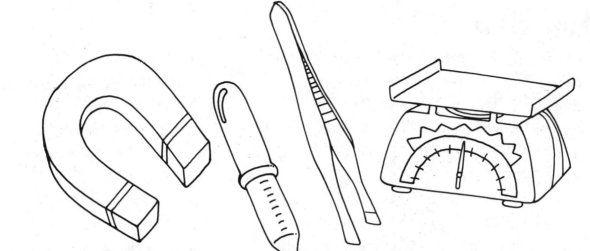

## Science Lab

- animals (ant farm, animals in cages, aquarium)
- assorted science manipulatives (seeds, plants, bones, batteries and wires, foil, etc.)
- blank cards
- collections (shells, nests, rocks, insects, leaves)
- display containers
- dissecting kits
- magazines
- magnets
- measuring tape
- microscopes
- paper trays (student work, record keeping)
- pencils (regular and colored)
- plastic jars
- paper plates and towels
- reference books
- resource charts
- rulers
- science photographs
- small science tools (magnifying glasses, specimen containers, eyedroppers, petri dishes, tweezers)
- sorting tubs or trays
- weighing scales

## Math Center

- calculators
- clocks (play and real)
- fraction models
- games and puzzles
- geoboards
- graph paper
- math manipulatives (beans, buttons, attribute and pattern blocks, play money, tangrams)
- measuring equipment (cups, spoons, rulers, yardsticks, metersticks, weighing scales)
- "real-life" activity supplies (restaurant menus, road maps, tax forms, situation cards)
- reinforcement activities (flash cards, computer programs)

## Wonderful World of Words (ABC/Word Center)

- ABC games, puzzles, and books
- alphabet cards
- blank index cards
- books about words and word origins (e.g., *Donovan's Word Jar* by Monalisa DeGroot)
- books containing alliterations, idioms, and figures of speech
- cards for labeling and sign-making
- class read-aloud selections
- class word jar or student-generated word bank
- core literature pieces
- flannel board and flannel-board letters
- magnetic letters
- paper trays (student work, record keeping)
- personalized spelling dictionaries
- pocket charts
- poetry books
- reference books (dictionaries, picture dictionaries, visualized dictionaries, glossaries from various subject areas, textbooks with glossaries)
- stick-on notepads
- student spelling journals
- wall dictionaries

## Social Studies Center

- atlases
- camera to document student-made displays
- compass
- crayons and markers
- film projector and film-strips
- games and puzzles
- globe
- historical artifacts and "realia"
- index cards for displays
- maps (new and old)
- paper
- pencil and pens
- picture file
- reference books (text-books, magazines, biographies, encyclopedias)
- reference charts
- stick-on notepads for labeling materials
- tape recorders and headsets
- theme-related display boards

## Listening Center and Recording Station

- blank cassette tapes
- books with read-along tapes
- crayons and markers
- paper
- pencils and pens
- poems and songs on tape
- skill tapes such as "how-to" tapes
- sound-effects materials
- tape recorders and headsets
- tape storage cabinet

## Computer Center

- basic computer equipment (computer, printer, paper)
- blank disks
- CD-ROM
- computer (VGA)-to-TV connector
- computer software
- disk storage units
- headsets
- modem
- on-line network service
- rolling cart (computer storage)
- storage shelves
- TV monitor

## Dramatic Play Center

- blankets and pillows
- cash register, order pad (restaurant playtime)
- child-sized furniture (stove, refrigerator, table, chairs, cupboard, bed, dresser)
- doll supplies (furniture, clothes, stroller, cradle)
- dolls of different ethnicities
- dress-up clothes (hats, aprons, purses, over-sized shirts and pants, ties, etc.)
- household items (mop, broom, duster, carpet sweeper, empty food boxes and cans, etc.)
- play workbench and tools (construction-work playtime)
- puppet stage
- puppets (sock, stick, marionettes)
- "real-life" play toys (plastic dishes, iron, foods, flowers, phone, etc.)

## Music Center

- books about composers and musicians
- music cassette tapes and CDs
- music pictures (instruments, notes, famous composers)
- musical instruments (store-bought and student-made)
- song sheets
- songbooks
- tape and/or CD player and headsets

## Cooking Club

- aprons and smocks
- books about famous cooks
- cleaning supplies
- cooking utensils, supplies, and equipment
- portable wooden towel rack
- recipe cards and cookbooks
- rolling cart with hot plate/microwave

## Repair Shop

- books about tools and related careers
- old appliances to dismantle and explore (toasters, clocks, radios, phones)
- tools (screwdrivers, hammers, pliers)

## Sewing Circle

- books about sewing and famous seamstresses and tailors
- cloth scraps
- crochet hooks, looms, knitting needles
- scissors
- sewing needles
- tape measure
- thread, yarn, ribbon

# Appendix D—Classroom Clean-Up Jobs

Needed classroom clean-up jobs will depend on factors such as your room arrangement, teaching style, student ages, and number of resource areas. Some jobs may require two students to finish the task quickly (3–5 minutes). Invite students to brainstorm additional jobs to add to the list.

## General Jobs

Can Carrier
Chalkboard Cleaner
Coat Clerk
Eraser Pounder

Lunch-Cart Keeper
Paper Manager(s)
Pencil Sharpener(s)
Sink Cleaner

Tabletop Dryer(s)
Tabletop Washer(s)
Trash Monitor

## Learning Centers

Art-Center Cleaner
Computer-Center Cleaner
History-Center Cleaner

Listening-Center Cleaner
Math-Center Cleaner
Music-Center Cleaner

Science-Center Cleaner
Writing-Center Cleaner

## Office Crew

Bulletin-Board Bailiff
Desktop Cleaner

Desktop-File Straightener
High-Tech Cleaner

## Reading Resource Area

Book-Box Bailiff
Maps Monitor

Pocket-Chart Checker
Poetry-Box Monitor

Shelf Straightener(s)

## Naturalists

Horticulturist (plants)
Marine Biologist (fish)
Zoologist (mammals)

# Appendix E—Generic File Labels

**Animals**

**Awards**

**Administrivia**
 Bulletins
 District
 Faculty Agendas
 Field Trips
 Guidelines
 Newsletters
 Order Forms
 Regulations
 Requisitions

**Basal Texts**

**Bulletin Boards**
 Fall
 Winter
 Spring
 Summer

**Calendars**

**Classroom Management**

**Communication**
 Parents
 Peers

**Computers**

**Creative Thinking**

**Critical Thinking**

**Curriculum**
 English/Language Arts
  Listening
  Reading
  Speaking
  Spelling
  Writing
 Fine Arts
  Art
  Music
 Health/Safety
  Family Life
  Nutrition
  Personal Hygiene
 Mathematics
  Application
  Computation
 Physical Education
  Motor Skills
  Physical Fitness
 Science
  Earth Science
  Life Science
  Physical Science
 Social Studies
  Geography
  Map Skills

**Discipline**

**Games**

**Goal Setting**

**Grade Level Meetings**

**Holidays**
 Halloween
 Thanksgiving
 Chanukah
 Christmas
 Valentine's Day
 St. Patrick's Day
 Easter
 Cinco de Mayo

**Pictures**

**Professional Growth**
 Peer Support
 Seminars
 Workshops
 Yearly Goals

**Seasonal Ideas**
 January
 February
 March
 April
 May
 June
 July
 August
 September
 October
 November
 December

**Story Starters**

# Annotated Bibliography

Alexander, Rosemary. *Instructor's Blockbuster Bulletin Boards.* Instructor Books, 545 Fifth Avenue, New York, NY 10017.

> This book is packed with ideas to enhance the learning environment of the classroom and get kids involved in the process. There are intriguing bulletin-board ideas in which basic boards remain constant as you add unique items to adapt displays throughout the year. This book also offers planning and design tips, ideas for special effects, and suggestions for stretching the space you have in your classroom.

Arcaro, Janice. *Creating Quality in the Classroom.* St. Lucie Press, 100 E. Linton Blvd., Suite 403B, Delray Beach, FL 33483.

> This book, written by a practicing teacher, is about acknowledging and building on current educational practices and making them even more successful.

Ballare, A., and Lampros, A. *The Classroom Organizer.* Parker Publishing Company, Business and Professional Division, A division of Simon and Schuster, West Nyack, NY, 10995.

> A unique collection of time and work savers for every facet of your job, including a variety of reproducible forms to organize your classroom, use with students, communicate with parents, and assist with professional growth and development.

Batzle, Janine. *Portfolio Assessment and Evaluation.* Creative Teaching Press, Inc., 10701 Holder St., Cypress, CA 90630.

> This book is filled with useful and practical information about assessment strategies that are part of classroom instruction and answers the questions teachers have about portfolio assessment. Includes a handy resource section.

Bosch, Karen A. and Kersey, Katharine C. *The First-Year Teacher, Teaching with Confidence (Gr. K–8).* NEA Professional Library, Box 509, West Haven, CT 06516.

> This book is designed as a practical, hands-on guide for the first-year teacher. It uses a self-help format, with useful suggestions to help new teachers throughout the school year.

Charles, C.M. *Elementary Classroom Management.* Longman, Inc., 95 Church Street, White Plains, NY 10601.

This comprehensive, well-organized guide covers virtually every aspect of classroom management. Helpful for both beginning and experienced teachers, it offers ways to cope more effectively with the innumerable daily tasks they face.

Christopher, Cindy J. *Nuts and Bolts Survival Guide for Teachers.* Technomic Publishing Company, Inc., 851 New Holland Avenue, Box 3535, Lancaster, PA 17604.

Motivating students to learn, meeting their diverse needs, and managing behavior are the paramount challenges facing teachers today. This book offers real, practical help to make the teaching experience more successful and rewarding.

Collis, Mark and Dalton, Joan. *Becoming Responsible Learners.* Heinemann Educational Books, Inc., 361 Hanover Street, Portsmouth, NH 03801.

This book skillfully combines the use of case studies, photographs, and examples of teacher-student dialogue to provide ways to meet the needs of students and help them perform and behave effectively and positively.

Holliman, Linda. *The Complete Guide to Classroom Centers.* Creative Teaching Press, Inc., 10701 Holder St., Cypress, CA 90630.

Everything a teachers needs to know about planning, creating, managing, and developing meaningful center activities. Detailed plans for 24 classroom centers for every reason and every season. Over 200 activities and ideas included.

Maeda, Bev. *The Multi-Age Classroom.* Creative Teaching Press, Inc., 10701 Holder St., Cypress, CA 90630.

This unique book describes a classroom where children of different ages, abilities, and needs learn at their own pace. It gives practical guidelines for integrating the curriculum, developing student independence, and involving parents in the classroom. Includes over 100 pages with reproducibles, photographs, and detailed descriptions of all curricular areas.

Mamchak, P. Susan and Steven R. *Teacher's Time Management.* Parker Publishing Company, West Nyack, NY 10995.

A much-needed resource that lets you handle time-consuming tasks, paperwork, and everyday situations quickly and efficiently, freeing your time to do what you do best—teach! Written for all grade levels, this practical guide contains over 250 reproducible forms, checklists, letters, and other ready-to-use techniques and time-saver tips.

Moran, Carol, et al., *Keys to the Classroom.* Corwin Press, Inc., A Sage Publications Company, 2455 Teller Road, Newbury Park, CA 91320.

With this book, beginning and experienced teachers discover how to set up a classroom environment. Tips and suggestions help teachers avoid common pitfalls and achieve goals more successfully.

Moss, Jeannette. *Learning Magazine's Superbook of Teacher Tips.* Learning Books, Springhouse Corporation, 1111 Bethlehelm Pike, Springhouse, PA 19477.

Within this book, you'll find more than 800 of the best tips, time savers, and curriculum ideas published in Learning Magazine over 18 years. All pointers have been revised, updated, and organized for easy reference.

Partin, Ronald L. *Classroom Teacher's Survival Guide.* The Center for Applied Research in Education, A division of Simon and Schuster, West Nyack, NY 10995.

This survival guide provides a smorgasbord of strategies and tips to solve the main problems facing teachers. Derived from actual teachers' experiences, it provides a range of practical options that can be adapted to fit your unique classroom situation.

Silver, Susan. *Organized to Be the Best!* Adams-Hall Publishing, P.O. Box 491002, Los Angeles, CA 90049.

This book offers suggestions and tips to help you develop an "action plan" for organizing your desk, work surfaces, drawers, paperwork, projects, filing cabinets, and storage areas. It contains many practical solutions to problems that may be holding you back.

Trisler, A. and Cardiel, P.H. *Managing Your Child-Centered Classroom.* Modern Learning Press, P.O. Box 167, Rosemont, NJ 08556.

> This book explains ways to manage a classroom through empowering students, encouraging them to actively seek knowledge, and giving them the independence to direct their own learning. Any teacher who believes in a child-centered approach to education will find this book full of useful, easy-to-implement ideas. Especially suited for grades first through fourth.

Williamson, Bonnie. *Classroom Management: A Guidebook for Success.* Dynamic Teaching Company, P.O. Box 276711, Sacramento, CA 95827.

> A step-by-step guide demonstrating how to use the Honor Incentive Program (HIP). It is a classroom recipe book to guide, give tips, and point the way to success in classroom management. The HIP system gives you the power to help students follow your lead through a democratic process encouraging team effort and creating an atmosphere of interpersonal respect.

Winston, Stephanie. *Stephanie Winston's Best Organizing Tips.* Simon and Schuster, Rockefeller Center, 1230 Avenue of the Americas, New York, NY 10020.

> This book is a cornucopia of solutions derived from the author's own experiences and the wealth of knowledge from other experts in the field. Each tip is a 60-second problem solver designed to enhance your productivity by helping you create a fun and functional physical environment that is pleasing to the eye.

Wong, Harry K. and Rosemary Tripi. *The First Days of School.* Harry K. Wong Publications, 1030 W. Maude Ave., Suite 507, Sunnyvale, CA 94086.

> *The First Days of School* will help all teachers jump-start and begin school successfully. It is designed to impact and sway the 40 percent of teachers who will leave the profession discouraged and overwhelmed. All teachers will benefit from this book, but it is a "must" for new teachers.

Dear Readers,

My mother, Phyllis Beams, is without exception the best teacher I have ever known. She taught me everything really important about teaching both at home and in the classroom.

As a student in my mother's classroom, I learned rigorous content with processes that stimulated and intrigued her students. We were given choice and support. She modeled the character, high expectations, perseverance, and responsible behavior expected of us.

Through me, my mother continues to influence teachers. Inherent in my management approaches are the moral underpinnings I learned from her. As a profession, we tend to let wonderful teachers pack up their boxes when they retire and leave without a trace. My hope is that you'll let me pass my mother's torch on to you and that you, too, will give your gifts to the next generation of teachers.

Our children must learn how to develop their individual potential while safeguarding liberty in a democratic republic. It is wonderfully gratifying to share with teachers some of the solutions I have learned for the complex management demands of today's classrooms. Classroom management is still the number-one factor connected to student achievement.

There are other people I must acknowledge, because without them, this book would never have been written. Many thanks and love to my sister, Anne Beams, friend and teacher "par excellence," who proofread every page and supplied an endless amount of feedback. Ed Lynn, my husband, offered ongoing support even through the most difficult times. Our children and grandchildren deserve much praise for their understanding hearts during the times when I put this project first.

Have a wonderful year of successful teaching!

Sincerely,

Alice Terry

Alice Terry

# Notes